WASTING MINDS

Praise for *Wasting Minds*

This book challenges the sacred cows of public education and seeks to change the way we think about schools. Ron Wolk offers logical, common-sense answers to the enormous educational problems facing us. Those responsible for finding solutions should pay close attention to what he says.

—*Stanley Goldstein*, founder and former CEO and Chairman of CVS Caremark Corporation

In the trench warfare surrounding school improvement that has raged for decades, Ron Wolk has worked as an embedded journalist who communicated to the rest of us how progress was lost and won. Reading *Wasting Minds* is like sitting at the feet of the sage of the movement as he separates the false from the true. The perspective he gives is invaluable.

—*Professor Clayton M. Christensen*, Harvard Business School and author of Disrupting Class *and* The Innovator's Dilemma

An architect friend of mine frequently complains that he has two kinds of clients: those with taste but no money, and those with money but no taste. His complaint has a rough parallel in education reform: those who really understand education have no power to change it, and those with the power to change it don't really understand it. If this latter group would take the time to read one book on education reform, it should be *Wasting Minds*.

—*Marion Brady*, former schoolteacher and university professor, book author, and education blogger for The Washington Post

Writing in the great tradition of such earlier critics of our lockstep high schools as Paul Goodman and Edgar Friedenberg, Ron Wolk argues persuasively that most adolescents need a much more personalized, customized form of education than our schools now provide. This is a highly readable personal account of Ron's own education from his perch at *Education Week* over most of the past three decades.

—*Robert B. Schwartz*, Academic Dean at Harvard University Graduate School of Education and Francis Keppel Professor of Practice of Educational Policy and Administration

SUSTAINABLE FORESTRY INITIATIVE
Certified Fiber Sourcing
www.sfiprogram.org

WASTING MINDS

WHY OUR EDUCATION SYSTEM IS FAILING

AND WHAT WE CAN DO ABOUT IT

RONALD A. WOLK

ASCD

Alexandria, Virginia USA

This book is dedicated to the past and present talented, hardworking members of the Education Week *staff who taught me much of what I know about education and continue doing so to this day.*

In the early 1970s, the United Negro College Fund conducted a public advertising campaign centered on the slogan "A mind is a terrible thing to waste." The slogan became part of the American vernacular. Sadly, evidence makes clear that the minds of millions of students of all races are still being wasted today.

1703 N. Beauregard St. • Alexandria, VA 22311-1714 USA
Phone: 800-933-2723 or 703-578-9600 • Fax: 703-575-5400
Website: www.ascd.org • E-mail: member@ascd.org
Author guidelines: www.ascd.org/write

Gene R. Carter, *Executive Director;* Judy Zimny, *Chief Program Development Officer;* Nancy Modrak, *Publisher;* Scott Willis, *Director, Book Acquisitions & Development;* Carolyn Pool, *Acquisitions Editor;* Julie Houtz, *Director, Book Editing & Production;* Miriam Goldstein, *Editor;* Reece Quiñones, *Senior Graphic Designer;* Mike Kalyan, *Production Manager;* Marlene Hochberg, *Typesetter;* Carmen Yuhas, *Production Specialist*

All web links in this book are correct as of the publication date below but may have become inactive or otherwise modified since that time. If you notice a deactivated or changed link, please e-mail books@ascd.org with the words "Link Update" in the subject line. In your message, please specify the web link, the book title, and the page number on which the link appears.

ASCD Member Book, No. FY11-5 (Feb. 2011, P). ASCD Member Books mail to Premium (P), Select (S), and Institutional Plus (I+) members on this schedule: Jan., PSI+; Feb., P; Apr., PSI+; May, P; July, PSI+; Aug., P; Sept., PSI+; Nov., PSI+; Dec., P. Select membership was formerly known as Comprehensive membership.

PAPERBACK ISBN: 978-1-4166-1131-8   ASCD product #111015
Also available as an e-book (see Books in Print for the ISBNs).

Quantity discounts for the paperback edition only: 10–49 copies, 10%; 50+ copies, 15%; for 1,000 or more copies, call 800-933-2723, ext. 5634, or 703-575-5634. For desk copies: member@ascd.org.

Library of Congress Cataloging-in-Publication Data

Wolk, Ronald A., author.
 Wasting minds : why our education system is failing and what we can do about it / Ronald A. Wolk.
     p. cm.
Includes bibliographical references and index.
ISBN 978-1-4166-1131-8 (pbk. : alk. paper)
 1. Educational change–United States. 2. Public schools–United States. I. Title.
LA217.2.W65 2010
370.973–dc22
                                2010043521

20 19 18 17 16 15 14 13 12 11   1 2 3 4 5 6 7 8 9 10 11 12

WASTING MINDS

WHY OUR EDUCATION SYSTEM IS FAILING

AND WHAT WE CAN DO ABOUT IT

| ACKNOWLEDGMENTS |

Thanks to . . .

Dennis Littky and Elliot Washor, founders of The Met School and Big Picture Learning, who put me on the board where I could see firsthand how education is supposed to work.

Ted Kolderie, Joe Graba, and Curt Johnson of Education/ Evolving, who sharpened my perspective by inviting me to participate in their exciting work and share their innovative ideas for how to improve schools.

Bob Schwartz, Mike Smith, Milbrey McLaughlin, and the Pew Forum on Standards-Based Reform, who gave me a decade of invaluable "professional development" and the opportunity during those years to realize that the dominant school-improvement strategy is off course.

Blake Hume Rodman and David Allan Kidd, two old *Teacher Magazine* buddies, who often challenged my opinions and sometimes even prompted me to change them.

Lauren Goldstein, who, as a graduate student at Brown, helped with fact-checking and research before heading home to New Orleans.

Finally, thanks to Jack, Kate, and Thomas Fitzgerald, my home-schooled neighbor children who run a pet care service and looked after my Yorkie puppy most mornings for many weeks so I could get some work done.

| PREFACE |

When we launched *Education Week* in September 1981, I, like most Americans, knew virtually nothing about elementary and secondary education. I had spent the previous 20 years as a university administrator—a decade at Johns Hopkins and another at Brown—and I thought about schools only when I was seeking one for my kids.

I left Brown in 1978 to become president and editor of Editorial Projects in Education, which had founded *The Chronicle of Higher Education* in 1966. My task was to find the next "big project." After a year's consideration, we decided on a "chronicle of lower education" because we became convinced that the public education system was about to enter a period of unprecedented ferment and controversy.

Student test scores had been declining for 20 years; one out of four students was leaving school without graduating; attendance rates in many urban schools were as low as 60 percent; and colleges and businesses were reporting that high school graduates were coming to them poorly prepared and in need of remedial courses.

To get a sense of whether a weekly newspaper was needed, my cofounder, Martha Matzke, and I talked with hundreds of people in the field and studied all the educational periodicals we could find. We were not impressed by what we saw or heard. People we interviewed generally said three things: (1) there is not enough news in education to justify a weekly; (2) education is local, and people in one state don't care what is going on in another state; and (3) people in public schools don't read, so at best we should consider a monthly newsletter that shunned charts and graphs in favor of cartoons.

We decided to publish *Education Week* despite the warnings because we believed that if the United States really was on the cusp of a revolution in public education, educators and policymakers would need comprehensive, accurate, objective, and timely information. No periodical was meeting that need at the time.

We soon discovered that the people we interviewed were wrong on two out of three claims. We found more than enough news, as well as a widespread and growing interest in education nationally. Unfortunately, the warning that too many people in public schools don't read—at least periodicals that deal with issues and policy, like *Education Week*—proved to be closer to the truth. Although there are more than 3 million teachers, more than 90,000 principals, about 14,000 superintendents, more than 100,000 school board members, and tens of thousands of people in administrative jobs throughout the system, *Education Week* subscriptions have hovered at just over 50,000 since the current school reform movement began in the early 1980s.

We were determined to make *Education Week* as independent, comprehensive, objective, and accurate as it is possible for a newspaper to be. We took no editorial positions but invited the opinions of others; I tried to keep my personal opinion to myself and, though that intention was sometimes frustrating, succeeded. Our only bias in publishing the new newspaper was the belief that public education is a social good.

Increasing Disillusionment

As the criticism of education mounted, I found myself feeling defensive. I have always believed that public schools play a vital role in a democratic society. And the criticism, it seemed to me, was unfair. After all, we were asking schools to fulfill a mission they were not designed for—educating all students to high levels, despite daunting socioeconomic and demographic challenges in a rapidly changing world.

With each passing year, as I came to understand the system and how it works, my sympathy for the plight of public schools eroded.

Schools, after all, are the institutions that society created to educate its young—not just white affluent kids, not just smart kids, but all children all the time. We have no adequate alternative system of public education and no alternative student body, so the schools we have must educate the children we have. And if schools can't transform themselves to carry out their mission successfully, then they should be replaced with new institutions that are designed for the task.

By the time I "retired" in 1997 and moved back to Rhode Island, I was so frustrated and disappointed that I fully expected to turn my attention to almost anything but education. Then, to my consternation, I was asked to serve on the board of Big Picture Learning. I'd never heard of it, but I agreed because the late Ted Sizer was chairman and I had admired him and his work for many years. I accepted, and that decision ended my brief retirement and set me on a new course in the reform of public education.

Big Picture was formed as a nonprofit organization in 1995 by Dennis Littky and Elliot Washor—two extraordinary and innovative leaders. They were senior fellows at the Annenberg Institute for School Reform at Brown University when Rhode Island chief state school officer Peter McWalters asked them to design a new state high school based on their educational philosophy.

The Metropolitan Career and Technical Academy ("The Met") opened in 1996 with a freshman class of 50 students. It was like no other high school in America—no classes, no courses, no grades, no common curriculum. Teachers are not traditional instructors but rather "advisors." An advisor stays with the same 15 students for the entire four years of high school. Students design their own individual education plan, which is anchored in an internship that takes them into the workplace two days a week to pursue something they are deeply interested in. In planning their personal curriculum, students work closely with their advisors, workplace mentors, and parents.

The Met was so successful in its first four years that it attracted international attention. Most of its students were disadvantaged minority students, many of whom were on the path to dropping out. All but a couple of students earned a diploma—they were often the first in their families to graduate from high school—and virtually every graduate entered a college or some other postsecondary program.

Tom Vander Ark, then education director of the Bill and Melinda Gates Foundation, was so impressed with The Met that he called it his "favorite high school in America" (Macris, 2000, p. 1C). Subsequently, a series of grants from Gates, beginning in 2000, has funded the creation of nearly 70 Big Picture schools in 18 states and several foreign countries.

Big Picture Learning restored my hope that we can create public schools that work. I had visited successful innovative public schools during my time at *Education Week*, like the Urban Academy and Beacon School in New York City, El Puente in Milwaukee, and Oyster School in Washington, D.C. But they were outliers—the exceptions that proved the rule. My involvement with Big Picture and the farsighted generosity of Gates convinced me that a movement to establish new, small, innovative schools that are different from each other and very different from conventional schools could well be the savior of public education in this country.

Increasing Frustration

So my journey did not end in 1997 as I had expected. It has just followed a radically different course. Consequently, my opinions have evolved and changed during the past decade, and, I hope, my understanding has deepened. It is customary for people to become more conservative as they age; I've become much more liberal—perhaps even radical. The more I learned about our system of public education, the more frustrated and angry I became. Then, when I joined Big Picture, I got a glimpse of what the future might be like if we had the wisdom, inventiveness, and courage to create it.

In 1999, I wrote a piece calling for the creation of a parallel system of public schools. I tried to get foundation support to create an organization to promote the idea. No takers. But my belief in the need for a new system of public schools has grown stronger.

This book is based on what I've learned about the public education system over the past 30 years. It is mostly a compendium of my opinions, but they are informed opinions that come from reading hundreds of books, papers, and reports (as well as almost every word in *Education Week* for more than 20 years), attending hundreds of meetings (often with the smartest people in the field), and visiting more than 120 schools (a few so good they literally made me weep and some so bad they literally made me weep). In short, I spent most of my waking hours for two decades thinking, reading, writing, and talking about public education.

I decided to write this book because I am appalled that so few people in society—from high-level policymakers to education leaders to parents and the public—understand the critical issues in education and the urgent need to put aside their preconceptions and challenge the conventional wisdom.

Eminent scholar and researcher John Goodlad recently put it this way:

> Over a period of sixty years, I have taught in a one-room school and school for delinquent boys, taught in every grade from the first through graduate school, been a dean for sixteen years, and studied in depth and breadth educational change, schooling, the education of educators, and more. I now look back in wonderment, anger, and near-despair at the stark reality of "we the people" scarcely murmuring for eight years over the imposition of the No Child Left Behind Act on our public schools. No powerful intellect is required for coming to the conclusion that we the people are grossly undereducated in what education is and negligent in the informed care of our irreplaceable asset, the public school. . . .
>
> I have concluded that we will never have the schools our democracy requires until their well-being is a major priority of local communities. *And we will not have them until policymakers, business roundtables, educational organizations, teacher-preparing institutions, and community leaders agree on what all schools are for.* The challenges are enormous, and unless we take them seriously and begin the necessary learning now, our century-old tinkering with schooling will continue. (Goodlad, 2009, para. 6, 7, emphasis added)

I have written this book because I share Goodlad's "wonderment, anger, and near-despair" and because the overriding purpose of my life is to help try to change the way Americans think about schools and education.

I realize that those who labor in the cause of better schools—many of them friends and colleagues—already know all this stuff, and most of them reject it. I don't expect to convert them, but I hope that the questions and arguments I raise at least give them pause. I also hope some of what I've written here finds its way into the public debate over education.

Mostly, I wrote this book for teachers, administrators, and opinion leaders who influence important decisions in society in all walks of life. I hope to reach some of those who shape education policy.

As I see it, Americans today face two overriding questions about education:

- *Can we get the schools we need simply by improving the ones we have?* Reluctantly, I have concluded that we can't.
- *How do we get from the schools we have to the schools we need?* I've written this book in the hope of providing at least a partial answer.

The old cliché is that pessimists see the glass half empty and optimists see the glass half full. I am neither. Regarding public education, I am an idealist: I see the glass as it is and can't accept the fact that it is not full.

May 2010

| INTRODUCTION |

At best, actions based on incorrect assumptions lead to ineffectiveness; at worst, they lead to failure.

We have known for a long time that our schools are in trouble. When the Soviet Union launched *Sputnik* half a century ago, politicians and educators declared that the United States was losing the race for space and called for immediate efforts to improve public schools. Laws were passed. Programs were funded. Curricula were revised. But no significant positive changes from that era have endured in public schools. The alarms, along with the so-called reform efforts they triggered, subsided as the United States quickly trumped the Soviets in space.

Some 25 years later, the alarms sounded again. Student test scores had been steadily declining for two decades, and dropout rates were unacceptably high. Japan was capturing the auto market and buying some of the nation's most prestigious office towers, like the Exxon Building in New York, Citicorp Center in San Francisco, and ARCO Plaza in Los Angeles, as well as the fabled Pebble Beach golf resort. Politicians and business leaders fretted about America's decline in the global economy, credited Japan's highly regimented and rigorous education for its success, and once again demanded better schools to make us more competitive.

The school reform movement that began in the early 1980s continues unabated to this day. It is driven mainly by the same rhetoric—that the United States must have the best schools in the world to win in the global economic competition—even though Japan long since entered a prolonged economic slump and U.S. business recovered without the aid of a rejuvenated education system.

Consequently, the United States, for a quarter-century, has been engaged in the most intensive effort in history to improve public education. Hundreds of blue-ribbon committees at every level of government and in the private sector have proposed solutions; policymakers have enacted thousands of laws and regulations; hundreds of billions of dollars have been spent on school reforms. Yet, despite this extraordinary effort, schools are not much better today than they were when we started.

Much Effort, Few Results

A nonprofit national security agency released a report in the fall of 2009 finding that 75 percent of Americans ages 17 through 24 (about 20 million people) are ineligible for military service—mainly because they didn't graduate from high school, have a criminal record, or are mentally or physically unfit (Davenport & Brown, 2009). Although the undeniable litany of failure is too long and too well known to repeat here, it can be captured in a few simple statistics:

- Approximately 25 of every 100 students drop out before graduating (Stillwell, 2010).
- In its latest report (2010), ACT found that only 24 percent of high schoolers who took the ACT were college-ready in all subject areas.
- In fall 2000, 28 percent of entering college freshmen enrolled in one or more remedial reading, writing, or mathematics courses (Parsad & Lewis, 2003).
- According to data gathered by the National Center for Education Statistics in 2008, only 55.9 percent of first-time full-time bachelor's degree–seeking students earned a degree within six years (National Center for Education Statistics, 2009b).

The message of those few statistics is that the majority of the young people who enroll in our public schools are poorly served—they either drop out or get a diploma but are not adequately prepared for college or work.

The cost of this failure in human and financial terms is staggering. Indeed, a business with such a record would go bankrupt, and it amazes me that millions of parents don't roar with outrage. One might even argue that this dismal situation exists because there is no outrage.

Why, despite great effort, have we made so little progress? Why does the problem even seem to get worse, no matter what we do? I believe it is because Americans, especially the decision makers and opinion leaders, cannot or will not set aside their special interests and deeply held biases about education to confront reality.

This is the case not only in education, but in most of the major issues confronting the United States today, including energy, for example. The presidential campaign of 2008 (and $4-a-gallon gasoline prices) raised the public's awareness of America's energy crisis and the dire consequences of continuing on our same course. This was not news; the energy crisis has been building for decades. We were warned by leaders and events on numerous past occasions of the enormous costs to our environment, our economy, and our national security that would result if we did not act decisively to end our dependence on carbon fuels and on foreign sources. Nearly 40 years ago, these rising concerns triggered the environmental movement and led to the establishment of the Environmental Protection Agency to address the issues of air and water pollution, toxic waste, and many other destructive effects of negligence and greed. But the Vietnam War ended and so did the spirit of protest that had, for a few short years, spoken "truth to power." Only in recent years have Americans come to realize that we absolutely must begin at once to change the way we think about energy. Now they need to realize that we must also begin at once to change the way we think about education.

Changing Our Thinking About Education

The energy crisis has reached the point that the dominant assumptions are now being questioned. We are beginning to understand that new thinking and bold action are required and that almost everything we do involving energy has to be radically changed.

Similarly, we must understand that the educational challenges facing the nation are every bit as daunting as those in energy, even though they do not alarm the public to the same degree. Radical thinking and action are just as critical if we are to provide our children with the schools they and the society so desperately need.

The two crises have much in common. Both threaten our welfare because we failed to anticipate the future and make the changes necessary to adapt to it.

Decisions in energy policy have been based on major assumptions that are not valid—assumptions such as these: we will always have enough carbon fuel so we don't need to invest in alternative energy sources; market forces will take care of the problem; putting restrictions on the energy industry will wreck the economy; the climate is simply going through a phase in the natural cycle and the planet will heal itself.

The major assumptions on which education policy has been based are equally invalid. That may sound like an arrogant exaggeration. After all, most of the people running our public education systems and leading the reform movement are knowledgeable, dedicated, and experienced. The vast majority of them support standards-based accountability, which has been the national education reform strategy of the past 20 years; they obviously believe the assumptions they hold are valid. Indeed, these assumptions are the widely accepted conventional wisdom, taken as gospel by most national and state leaders. That, however, doesn't make them any more correct than the assumptions underlying energy policy that have been so widely accepted by smart people. "We simply assume that the way we see things is the way they really are or the way they should be," says Stephen R. Covey, international authority on leadership and acclaimed author and consultant, "and our attitudes and behaviors grow out of these assumptions" (2004, p. 24).

That set of assumptions, attitudes, and behaviors is at the root of our educational crisis, and therein also lies a solution if one is ever to be found.

A Misdiagnosis of the Problem

The dominant assumptions in education are invalid mainly because they result from a misdiagnosis of the problem. Many of our leaders believe the system is essentially sound and only needs to be ratcheted up. They reject the argument that the education system is so obsolete and out of synch with the rapidly changing world that nothing short of a substantial redesign can create the schools we need.

Most of our leaders at every level have been wrong on both energy and education. They resist and deny reality because it is so difficult to accept and frightening to contemplate. The issues are so complex and controversial that people find it more expedient to accept most of the system as a given and pursue reforms that are incremental and marginal. They are convinced that a major overhaul of the system would wreak political havoc and disrupt the education of millions of children. In the face of such dire possibilities, why take chances with radical change?

Finally, efforts to overhaul or redesign the education system are fiercely resisted because the status quo is so firmly entrenched and the culture of public schools is so deeply embedded. School boards, administrators, and teachers are not bad people who want schools to fail, but they feel compelled to protect their routines, their status, and their turf, and they weave a rationale to justify that.

Because the reform strategy has been based on flawed assumptions, it has been driving the education system in the wrong direction; and the further it goes, the more difficult it will be to get it on the right course—if that is even possible. And because the assumptions are so widely accepted, they represent an almost insurmountable obstacle to doing what must be done to improve the existing public schools, let alone create new and different ones.

That situation is unfortunate and dangerous. An effective education system is, in many ways, a prerequisite to finding solutions to all of the other formidable problems the nation faces. Without it, where will we get the people, the ideas, the creativity, and the technology needed to meet the challenges and seize the opportunities of this new century?

We certainly will not get the schools we need if we don't challenge the assumptions on which our education reform strategies and policy decisions have been based. The main purpose of this book is to do exactly that. In Part 1, I examine these major assumptions and try, using facts and logic, to show that they are invalid. In Part 2, I offer the assumptions on which an *effective* school system should be based.

The following assumptions, on which virtually all school reform efforts are based, are so flawed that they lead to action that is ineffective at best and counterproductive at worst:

- Students are not performing adequately because they and their teachers don't work hard enough. The solution is a "get-tough" policy like No Child Left Behind.
- The key to improving student performance and closing the achievement gap is to establish rigorous content standards and a core curriculum for all schools—preferably on a national basis.
- Standardized test scores provide an accurate measure of student learning and should be used to determine promotion and graduation.
- The United States should require all students to take algebra in the 8th grade and higher-order math in high school largely in order to increase the number of scientists and engineers and thus make us more competitive in the global economy.
- We need to put a highly qualified teacher in every classroom to deliver an excellent education to every student and improve our schools.
- Having an effective principal in every school would make the difference between a school that works and one that doesn't.
- The student dropout rate can be reduced by dropout-prevention programs and by raising the mandatory attendance age from 16 to 18.
- Making the school day and school year longer will increase student learning.
- If we invest more money in public schools, we will be able to provide every student with an excellent education.

The statement that opened this Introduction bears repeating: At best, actions based on incorrect assumptions lead to ineffectiveness; at worst, they lead to failure.

Research: A Weak Reed

In education, we almost always cite research to buttress our opinions. I do that in this book, even though I know that one can find some research to support almost any opinion. In science, we demand empirical evidence to support our conclusions; in the social sciences, not so much. I once believed that education research would lead us to the promised land of successful schools and high student achievement. I no longer believe that.

Virtually all research on student achievement and school quality is based on standardized test scores. If test scores are not a fair, accurate, or reliable measure of student learning, then the research and its conclusions are flawed and unreliable.

Moreover, because there is so much room for subjective interpretation of data in education research, the findings often cancel each other out (especially for those who want to use them to justify decisions). For example, some research insists that money doesn't matter, but some concludes that it does. Vouchers work; no they don't. Learning is more likely in small classes; no it isn't. And on and on. This plethora of research and data provides cover for those who make policy or pronouncements, allowing them to choose the research that supports their preconceived notions.

In this book, I am compelled to cite research that embodies the very faults I just mentioned. That is because research based on test scores is the coin of the realm and is demanded as evidence for action. Equally important, that's about all there is. Would that we had longitudinal research to show effects over time of one approach versus another.

Lacking reliable research findings, much of what I argue is based on personal observations, logic, and common sense. For example, it makes sense, at least to me, that students will learn more if they are motivated to learn, and that they will be more motivated to learn if they have some freedom in deciding what they will learn. It makes no sense, at least to me, that the dropout rate can be reduced by requiring students to stay in school for another year or two. If a failing student has decided when he turns 16 that staying in school is futile, then extending his sentence by another year or two is cruel and unusual punishment and only delays the inevitable.

As we try to evaluate contradictory assertions, we must also ask the following questions: Where should the burden of proof lie? Should those who question the conventional school model and propose significant change be required to prove in advance that their proposals will accomplish the desired goal?

It makes more sense, at least to me, that those who resist significant change and continue to pursue the current strategy of standards-based accountability be required to prove that it is accomplishing its goals. Instead, in the face of little or no real progress, they argue that doing the same, more intensively and on a national basis, will solve the problem.

I can't prove that the changes recommended in this book will produce the kinds of schools we need. But I can prove, using the metrics accepted by the architects and supporters of the current reform strategy, that the strategy has not worked after nearly two decades of effort. Indeed, the conventional school is obsolete and may very well be beyond repair. It doesn't work for a significant majority of the young people who are required to attend it and never really has. How else do we explain the fact that nearly one-third of the students flunk out or drop out and fewer than half of those who graduate are adequately prepared for either college or the modern workplace?

PART 1

FLAWED ASSUMPTIONS

| CHAPTER 1 |

The "Get-Tough" Policy

ASSUMPTION: *Students are not performing adequately because they and their teachers don't work hard enough. The solution is a "get-tough" policy like No Child Left Behind.*

The belief in a "get-tough" policy is the legacy of *A Nation at Risk*, the sensational federal report published in 1983 that warned Americans that their public schools were being inundated by "a rising tide of mediocrity." In headline-making rhetoric, it declared, "If an unfriendly foreign power had attempted to impose on America the mediocre educational performance that exists today, we might well have viewed it as an act of war." "History is not kind to idlers," the report scolded, and declared that the nation had lost sight of the "high expectations and disciplined effort" needed for successful schools (National Commission on Excellence in Education, 1983, p. 1).

Though widely praised, the report was mostly a misguided diagnosis of the nation's educational malaise. Its major assumption was that U.S. schools were essentially sound, that student performance had declined because we lowered our standards. To improve, we needed higher standards that would demand that everybody work harder and reach higher. That assumption drove the school reform movement in the wrong direction from the outset by placing highest priority on standards, testing, and hard work.

A Nation at Risk completely missed the real reasons for the poor performance of America's students and schools. It did not even mention poverty, race, urban schools, new immigrants, or the impact of popular culture, all of which are major contributing causes of most of today's educational problems. It did not even question the way today's schools are organized and operated or whether they have not changed to keep up with the times.

The report's greatest contribution was that it created an opportunity for a much overdue assessment of the purpose and goals of public education in a democracy and the structure and culture of public schools. For the most part, the opportunity presented by *A Nation at Risk* was squandered. Instead, the nation rushed to action with little thought or analysis.

During the years immediately after the report, every state created blue-ribbon committees; governors claimed education to be their highest priority and declared themselves to be "education governors." States and districts pushed through reforms, many of which were ineffective and short lived. Before long, critics began describing the reform movement as "Ready, fire, aim!"

In 1988, *The Forgotten Half* was published, placing the focus on the students ignored in the federal study—those who were being deprived of the right to a good education and a chance to attend and succeed in college. Several reports followed calling for "systemic" change and noting that virtually every part of the current system needed repair.

If We Only Worked Harder

Despite the reports, the notion persisted that much of our problem would be solved if only teachers and students worked harder. Nearly two decades after *A Nation at Risk*, the U.S. Congress passed No Child Left Behind (NCLB)—the omnibus law based at least partly on the assumption that students and teachers are not succeeding because they aren't trying hard enough. When Senator Ted Kennedy and Representative George Miller joined President George W. Bush to introduce No Child Left Behind in Congress, I was appalled. I wrote a column in *Teacher Magazine* expressing my concern:

> The proposal to test grades 3 through 8 every year would be bad policy that could create chaos and harm thousands of children without improving student performance. . . . People who should know better are supporting the Bush testing plan, because they believe it will force

teachers to raise their expectations for poor and minority students and prompt them to teach those kids the rigorous curriculum that high-achieving students get. . . . President Bush has justified these tests by saying that "Without yearly testing we do not know who is falling behind and who needs our help." If that's what this is all about, we can save lots of time and money. All the President and the Congress need to do is go to the districts and schools that serve the urban and rural poor, immigrants, and racial minorities. They can see with their own eyes the children who we always leave behind and who desperately need our help. And if they need more testing to tell them that, then they haven't been paying attention. (Wolk, 2001, p. 4)

I was in a small minority.

Shortly after NCLB was enacted, I attended a meeting of the Gates Foundation education advisory committee with Sandy Kress, senior advisor to President Bush on education and an avid proponent of the No Child Left Behind Act of 2001. He has been described as "the great architect of the great train wreck" (Schools Matter, 2006). Kress asserted that a primary purpose of NCLB was to get tough with school administrators and teachers and let them know that they would be held accountable for their failure to close the achievement gap.

To overcome this perceived laziness and incompetence, NCLB emphasized accountability and mandated penalties for schools that failed to meet specified goals for adequate yearly progress (AYP) in closing the student achievement gap. In 2008, 10 percent of the nation's public schools had failed to meet AYP requirements for six consecutive years and faced mandatory restructuring or closure—the most severe sanction of the law. And many thousands more were put on track to restructuring.

Blame Students, Blame Teachers

Closing the student achievement gap is a worthy objective, as is the effort to increase the commitment of teachers and students to teaching and learning. But to assume that the problem of poorly performing schools and students can be solved with threats and penalties is to misunderstand both the institution and the people in it and to further widen the achievement gap.

A study by the Advancement Project (2010), an organization of veteran civil rights lawyers, found that get-tough policies like zero tolerance and high-stakes testing have "turned schools into hostile and alienating environments for many of our youth, effectively treating them as drop-outs-in-waiting" (p. 8). The end result of these policies is a "school-to-prison pipeline," in which students throughout the country are "treated as if they are disposable, routinely pushed out of school and toward the juvenile and criminal justice systems" (p. 8).

A dramatic rise in school-based arrests coincided with the passage of NCLB, according to the report, which noted that "at the national level, there were almost 250,000 more students suspended out-of-school in 2006–07 than there were just four years earlier, when NCLB was signed into law" (p. 20). And the number of students expelled during this time rose by 15 percent.

There is no denying that too many students are unmotivated and unengaged; they find schools boring at best and alien places at worst. Even many capable students from reasonably affluent families do only what's needed to get the grades necessary for admission to college. In schools populated by such students, the senior year is viewed largely as a waste of time because they've submitted their college applications and their subsequent performance won't be considered.

There are undoubtedly teachers who retired long ago and didn't tell anybody. Indeed, as I write this, an organization of students in Providence, Rhode Island, announced the results of a survey of 1,700 students and 149 teachers. The survey found that "too many teachers rely on ditto sheets or other hand-outs instead of teaching, and the practice of students reading textbooks in class is common." In focus groups, 44 percent of students said their teachers don't motivate them, and some reported that teachers actually discouraged them from trying harder. Students complained that a social studies teacher "called me stupid in front of the whole class," and another teacher said, "Why don't you just drop out?" Other comments attributed to teachers were "I don't care if you graduate; I still get paid" and "If you want to fail, fail quietly" (Borg, 2009, para. 1, 2, 3, 7, 10). Even the city's premier high school was found wanting. Students reported that teachers rely on lectures rather than hands-on learning and said that faculty members often fail to make their subjects relevant to the real world.

It is neither fair nor true, however, to claim that these complaints apply to most or even many teachers. And it is hard to believe that even the incompetent teachers go to work every day determined to teach badly and disrespect their students.

By blaming poor student performance on teacher laziness or incompetence, we will surely forge solutions that do not address the real problem. Students are failing to get the education they need to succeed in an ever-changing world largely because many of them are weighed down by the baggage of poverty and broken homes and arrive at school woefully unprepared for formal education.

A College Board report cited "overwhelming barriers" for such students, especially males. Gaston Caperton, former governor of West Virginia and president of the College Board, said the report describes "young men who are so far removed from our opportunity culture that they almost have no hope of contributing to our social and our economic growth. As a result, they live in despair, hopelessness, and too often violence and incarceration" (Roach, 2010, para. 3).

If these students are unprepared for school, the school is even less prepared for them. Most teachers find it difficult, if not impossible, to reach these kids. Teacher preparation programs didn't preview the reality they would face. The structure and culture of the conventional school model are incompatible with most of today's students, and the model does not address their problems and needs.

It should not surprise us that many youngsters fail and drop out or barely graduate from high school, and that more than half of those who do enter college leave without getting a degree. They have been on the path to failure for most of their lives, and schools don't have the knowledge, the power, or the motivation to redirect them. No Child Left Behind intended to focus on the plight of the disadvantaged, but its emphasis on increased testing and accountability has probably widened the educational gulf between the haves and have-nots.

In March of 2010, President Obama sent Congress an education plan that would essentially defang NCLB. Most important, the president's plan would end the provision that gives schools pass-fail grades and instead would judge schools on measures like attendance, graduation rates, and learning environment rather than simply test scores. The emphasis is on measuring individual students' academic growth, Mr. Obama said. The president called for an end to the NCLB provision that required schools not meeting the testing benchmarks for two consecutive years to provide busing to other schools for students wishing to transfer. His plan would remove the impossible mandate that every student be proficient in reading and math by 2014. But he replaced it with the goal of having all students graduate ready for college by 2020 (Dillon, 2010).

The Obama plan was hardly out of the box when the criticisms began. It was seen as unfair to teachers, still too reliant on tests, a retreat from ensuring good education as a civil right, a weakening of standards, and heavy-handed federal interference.

The new plan does have vexing problems, but it is a substantial improvement on NCLB and takes an important step away from the get-tough approach.

| CHAPTER 2 |

All Standards for All Students

ASSUMPTION: *The key to improving student performance and closing the achievement gap is to establish rigorous content standards and a core curriculum for all schools—preferably on a national basis.*

The get-tough strategy of school improvement rests on the premise that high standards, rigorous curricula, high-stakes tests, and threats to withhold funding from poorly performing schools will lead to better schools and higher student achievement as measured by test scores. Those committed to this reform strategy believe the bar must be raised, and students and teachers must meet more rigorous requirements or be penalized.

Although standards-based accountability has been the national school reform strategy for nearly two decades, it gained momentum from the passage of No Child Left Behind. Opposition to NCLB has steadily grown since its inception, even among early supporters, but the drive for higher common standards and more rigorous courses and tests continues unabated. Prominent business leaders, politicians, and education policymakers have made national standards, curriculum, and testing a high priority.

These admonitions have a kind of Orwellian ring. More than two decades ago, proponents of standards-based accountability promoted it as the solution to mediocre education and poor schools. Based on the results of the strategy, one must wonder how they can argue so forcibly that it is still the right reform but only needs to be ratcheted up to be successful. Even based on their own (flawed) measure of test scores, the dismal record speaks for itself.

The scores on the National Assessment of Educational Progress remain dismally low, and almost 30 percent of the nation's public schools have been designated as low-performing under No Child Left Behind. An article published in *Education Week* reported that

> almost 30,000 schools in the United States failed to make adequate yearly progress under NCLB in the 2007–08 school year. For states with comparable data for the 2006–07 school year, the number of such schools increased by 28 percent.
>
> Half those schools missed their achievement goals for two or more years, putting almost one in five of the nation's public schools in some stage of a federally mandated process designed to improve student achievement. The number facing sanctions represents a 13 percent increase for states with comparable data over the 2006–07 school year.
>
> Of those falling short of their academic-achievement goals, 3,559 schools—4 percent of all schools rated based on their progress—faced the law's more serious interventions in the 2009–10 school year. That's double the number that were in that category one year ago. (Hoff, 2008, para. 1–3)

Standards-based accountability has been widely embraced because there is a certain logic to it: decide what every student should know and be able to do; formulate a "rigorous" curriculum to ensure that students get the designated knowledge and skills; use standardized tests to assess them yearly to make sure they are succeeding; punish them and the schools if they fail to meet the standards.

In business, a similar approach is called the "virtuous circle," or feedback loop, and it is used in producing things like autos and computers. Set high-quality standards, develop procedures to see that the standards are met; check them for quality at several stages of production; feed results back into the system so it can be improved.

That made sense to me in the early years. I became a member of the Pew Forum on Standards-Based Reform, a group of the nation's finest minds in education, including Mike Smith and Jennifer O'Day, whose scholarly papers prompted standards-based reform. The forum met for a couple of days four times a year to visit schools and study and discuss reform efforts. Although I found every meeting stimulating and an exercise in "professional development," I became increasingly skeptical about standards-based reform as a strategy to improve schools.

Standards Don't Educate Students

I came to realize that standards don't prepare students for anything; they don't educate kids or improve teaching. Standards are a framework of expectations and educational objectives. A car company can have high-quality standards for its product, but if it lacks the organization, procedures, and a properly trained workforce necessary to achieve them, the standards aren't worth much. High standards don't guarantee quality, as Toyota's troubles in the winter of 2009–10 painfully demonstrated.

States have spent nearly 20 years formulating 21st century standards for a 19th century school system. The conventional school model is incapable of meeting these standards. It is not properly organized, its procedures are outmoded, and its workforce is not trained for the job. Moreover, a significant number of the students (the potential market) are unable to meet the standards and are unwilling even to try.

We will make real progress only when we realize our problem in education is not mainly one of performance but one of design. It is the obsolete and flawed design of the conventional public school that accounts for the poor performance of a great many students.

My experience with the Pew Forum also convinced me that while standardization and uniformity may work with cars, they don't work for the young people we saw on those many school visits. Today's students are the most diverse in history. They come from different socioeconomic situations and different cultures. They learn at different rates and in different ways, have different problems, talents, and aspirations. Imposing more standardization and uniformity on them is counterproductive.

To insist that all students be treated the same way, that they all study the same subject at the same time in the same way, is a strategy that denies reality. It is like a physician stepping into his waiting room and telling the assembled patients, "It's Monday morning; everyone gets a shot of penicillin." That prescription wouldn't work for most of the patients and might actually harm some. Inflexible standards-based accountability doesn't work for most of our young people and harms some of them.

In his best-selling book *Disrupting Class*, business professor and consultant Clayton Christensen writes:

> The current educational system—the way it trains teachers, the way it groups students, the way the curriculum is designed, and the way the school buildings are laid out—is designed for standardization. If the nation is serious about leaving no child behind, it cannot be done by standardized methods. Today's system was designed at a time when standardization was seen as a virtue. It is an intricately interdependent system. Only an administrator suffering from virulent masochism would attempt to teach each student in the way his or her brain is wired to learn within this monolithic batch system. Schools need a new system. (Christensen, Horn, & Johnson, 2008, p. 11)

Off Course from the Outset

The original proposals for standards-based accountability in the late 1980s advocated that standards be "parsimonious," limited to the basic, organizing concepts in a discipline, and not correlated with each grade. The original advocates recommended that students be tested at the 4th, 8th, and 12th grades to measure progress, and that students who needed more time to meet the standards should get it. That was a new concept in public education that challenged the rigid school schedule by making time the variable and learning the constant. Finally, and perhaps most important, the founders of standards-based reform pressed for equal-opportunity standards to guarantee that all students would have an equal chance to learn what they would be assessed on.

Common standards may work at the elementary school level— which, by the way, is the part of the system where standards have gained the most traction. To be successful and productive adults, all students must learn to read, write, listen, and speak, to master basic arithmetic, and to get introduced to the world around them— the arts, science, history, and so on. The designation "elementary" makes the point.

Beginning with middle school, specific, high, common standards of what *every* student should know and rigorous common curricula are incompatible with the needs and interests of a diverse student body. A budding poet does not need to know quadratic equations any more than an emerging physicist needs to know the world of Victorian poetry. After elementary school, the standards and the process of meeting them must be tailored to the students.

Marion Brady, a former columnist for the *Orlando Sentinel*, is now writing an education column for the *Washington Post*. He recently penned a commentary about standards in *Education Week* in which he uses an apt and amusing analogy to make his point.

After watching a border collie put on an amazing display of sheep herding in Scotland, he found himself thinking about standards. Border collies are bred to do their job, and they're great at it. But if you're lost in a snowstorm, you don't need a border collie; you want a big strong dog that functions well in the snow—like a Saint Bernard. To keep varmints from killing your chickens, a fox terrier is better than a Saint Bernard. Brady writes that there are all kinds of things dogs can do:

> Want to sniff luggage for bombs? Chase felons? Stand guard duty? Retrieve downed game birds? Guide the blind? Detect certain diseases? Locate earthquake survivors? Entertain audiences? Play nice with little kids? Go for help if Little Nell falls down a well? With training, dogs can do those jobs well.

> So, let's set performance standards and train all dogs to meet them. All 400 breeds. Leave no dog behind! Two-hundred-pound Mastiffs may have a little trouble with the chase-the-fox-into-the-hole standard, and Chihuahuas will probably have difficulty with the tackle-the-felon-and-pin-him-to-the-ground standard. But, hey, standards are standards! No excuses! No giving in to the soft bigotry of low expectations. Hold dogs accountable.

> Here's a question: Why are one-size-fits-all performance standards inappropriate to the point of silliness when applied to dogs, but accepted without question when applied to kids? (Brady, 2009, para. 8–10)

In other words, how can we foist upon our kids what we wouldn't do to a dog?

Like most reasonable ideas in education, the standards movement was badly implemented from the start. Mainly for political and financial reasons, opportunity-to-learn standards were rejected almost immediately; detailed grade-level content standards have been established; students are tested constantly; the school schedule is now even more inflexible.

Flawed Logic

Proponents justify their ardent support of tougher standards and more testing by insisting that it is a matter of civil rights. They argue that to expect and demand less of black and Hispanic students, too many of whom are academically at risk, is discriminatory and deprives them of an equal education. In a rare burst of eloquence, President George W. Bush called it "the soft bigotry of low expectations."

Civil rights leaders with indelible (and, sadly, even recent) memories of blacks and Latinos being relegated to poor schools and the lowest academic tracks have generally accepted this argument. They want minority students to receive an education equal to that of whites, which means that they must be held to the same standards as whites.

The intent is praiseworthy, but the logic is flawed.

The issue is surely one of civil rights. Minority students have the right to equal educational opportunity. But the existing public education system does not provide that. Neither does the current strategy of standards-based accountability. It demands that minorities perform at the same high level as whites but offers them an education inferior to that of whites.

A disproportionate percentage of minority students are often trapped in bad schools and taught by less competent and less experienced teachers. They are expected to master a content-heavy curriculum rooted in a culture that has largely tried to exclude them.

Various studies have concluded that nonschool factors are the most powerful influence of student achievement. Some have suggested that family characteristics account for as much as 75 percent of achievement.

The Educational Testing Service recently updated its 2003 report (*Parsing the Achievement Gap*) that looked at "the correlation between life experiences and life condition on the one hand and [between] cognitive development and school achievement on the other" (Barton & Coley, 2009, p. 2). Basically, the report identified 16 factors that correlate with student achievement. Seven are school factors, like teacher preparation and class size; one is parent involvement; and eight focus on correlates in the child's environment, like hunger and nutrition, frequent changing of schools, and parental effect on early literacy.

Many, if not most, of the students at the lower end of the achievement gap are minority students who come from single-parent homes and live below or near the poverty line. Unlike their more affluent peers, their environment has not prepared them for school, and because they are not ready (and the schools are not ready for them), they tend to fall further and further behind and become mired in a culture of failure. By the 4th grade, many are on their way to dropping out.

Systematic discrimination against minorities and the poor for most of our history has created the achievement gap and has put millions of young people at an enormous disadvantage. And it continues to this day. Despite the Supreme Court's ban on segregated schools more than half a century ago, most minority students are confined to predominantly minority schools that are of lower quality than predominantly white schools. Studies show that even middle-class African American students generally do not perform as well as their white peers because of formidable barriers to academic and personal development.

The fact is that equality in education remains more of a hope than a reality. Civil rights leaders need to realize that until a high-quality education is available to all minority children, standards-based accountability is a form of discrimination. And policymakers and educators must recognize and acknowledge that an achievement gap will exist as long as out-of-school conditions are not addressed effectively.

The dominance of nonschool factors notwithstanding, we can't let schools off the hook. Because school factors have a considerable effect on student achievement, the gap can be partially closed by schools, but only if the educational system adapts to the reality of disadvantaged students and their needs. If schools have the potential to achieve even a 25 percent improvement in student learning, then we should accept nothing less. That level of improvement would be a major step toward narrowing the achievement gap.

The Influence of College Admission Requirements

To criticize standards-based accountability as a failed strategy is not to argue that standards are not important. Neither Professor Christensen nor I would argue that standards are unnecessary. Schools without standards are unacceptable, and society should indeed hold high expectations for all students. But those expectations should reflect the values of the family and society and not simply the archaic academic demands of college admission offices. And in this age when the mantra is college for all, admission requirements are driving standards to a large degree.

Abraham Flexner is famous for his study that looked at professionalized medicine in the late 1800s. But he also wrote a book called *The American College*, in which he declared that college admission requirements have influenced high schools by "practically determining for them the spirit, method, and contents of their instruction" (1908, p. 63). The high school, he insisted, is "now largely controlled by the college in its interest" (p. 64). And he added that the negative effect of that control filters down through the elementary school.

Flexner argued that "narrowly intellectualistic admission machinery" makes precollegiate education "a narrow, monotonous grind" (p. 98). If he were here today, Flexner might well conclude that national academic standards and a national curriculum would be a complete capitulation to those "narrowly intellectualistic" college admission requirements.

His concerns are as valid today as they were more than a century ago. Rona Wilensky, former principal of Mount Vista High School in Boulder, Colorado, wrote in *Phi Delta Kappan* a few years ago:

> If it is the hyper-academic focus of college entrance requirements that leads to the success of only a few, the outright failure of others, and

the low achievement of many in our K–12 system, then further tightening the alignment between colleges and public schooling can only make things worse. . . . And by keeping our attention focused on what has seemed to work in the past rather than on what is needed for the future, we run the further risk of missing a current political opportunity to actually remake the landscape of education in a way that will prepare students for the new demands of the globalized economy and interdependent world. (Wilensky, 2007, p. 249)

Obviously, hers is not the prevailing opinion. States, districts, businesses, and foundations are putting great emphasis on the need to prepare every child for college. The flawed assumption is that preparing kids to meet college admission requirements ensures that they will have been well educated and are ready to face the future. Not so.

The main purposes of schools should be to help students prepare to be successful and productive adults and lifelong learners—to help them develop good habits of mind and behavior; to learn to reason—to gather information, organize it logically, evaluate it, and use it effectively. We should certainly demand that all students strive to meet those standards by showing up for school, working hard and doing their best, respecting their teachers and peers, and obeying the rules. Those are the high expectations of good citizenship and productive workers.

In return, students have a right to expect their school to provide an appropriate learning environment and an equal opportunity to learn; to do its best to accommodate their differences, recognize their strengths and weaknesses and the influence of their out-of-school environment; to treat them as individuals and help them adapt to the challenges of schooling. These students deserve better than to be force-fed the one-size-fits-all education of the conventional school.

If we want to make real progress in closing the achievement gap, we need to shift our emphasis from standardizing schools to redesigning them. The school of tomorrow must put students first and educate them one at a time. And like setting standards that match the diversity of dog breeds, standards should set expectations that coincide with the diverse talents and interests of students.

A rigorous national core curriculum linked to national common academic standards inevitably cements in place the educational orthodoxy that characterizes America's schools. The National Governors Association, the Council of Chief State School Officers, more than 40 states, and other education, political, business, and philanthropic leaders are well on their way to agreeing on common standards in the near future. But even if the common standards are well thought out, are better than most existing state standards, and are enthusiastically embraced by all of the states, they are not likely to achieve their goal. Covering every grade, they fail the test of parsimony that the original standardistas proposed. The math standards in the upper grades will still be largely out of reach of kids who did not learn in the earlier grades because of lack of interest or poor teaching. But most of all, too much is likely to be lost in the process of implementation. What policymakers mandate rarely survives the journey to the classroom intact.

Perhaps a case could be made for common *K–6* standards *limited* to English and math, but common standards and curriculum beyond that will stifle even the most modest efforts to personalize education.

Curriculum is the engine of our public education system. It shapes to a large degree how schools spend money, the way they use time, and the assignment (and preparation) of teachers. Curriculum, standards, and standardized tests are inextricably linked, and they determine how students spend their 15,000 hours or so of schooling.

Despite its importance, the specific content of curriculum doesn't get much attention from parents, politicians, or the media, except for calls for more rigorous courses and more math and science. Although today's curriculum is rooted in the early part of the last century, nearly everybody somehow believes it is adequate to prepare our children for the 21st century.

Instead of just demanding more "rigor" and more math and science, we would be better off asking: What is the main purpose of the curriculum? Is it to designate specific knowledge that every student must master? Or is it mainly to provide content that is necessary to the process of learning to think constructively about specific issues and problems?

The answers to those questions are profoundly important in determining what we expect of our public schools and our students. If the main purpose of the curriculum is to designate specifically what every student should know, then the standards movement and core curriculum may make some sense. If the purpose is mainly to provide an essential component in learning to think and solve problems, then requiring all kids to learn the same things at the same time makes little sense.

In an *Education Week* commentary a few years ago, before his treatise on dog breeds, Marion Brady challenged the traditional curriculum more directly when he wrote the following:

> Of all the education-related unexamined assumptions, none is more deeply embedded than the belief that the main business of schooling is to teach the "core curriculum"—math, science, social studies, and language arts. . . . School, finally, isn't about disciplines and subjects, but about what they were originally meant to do—help the young make more sense of life, more sense of experience, more sense of an unknowable future. And in that sense-making effort, math, science, social studies, and language arts simply aren't up to the challenge. They've given us a curriculum so deeply flawed it's an affront to the young and a recipe for societal disaster. (Brady, 2006, para. 5, 7)

And Professor William G. Wraga of the University of Georgia reminds us that "academic subjects were developed to discover knowledge, not to disseminate it" (2009, pp. 88–89).

Critics of a national common curriculum are scolded for demeaning the value of knowledge. Even wild-eyed liberals like me know that learning to think and reason is impossible without knowledge. But it is arrogant and counterproductive to assume that some panel of experts should decide what every child should know (beyond elementary school). Maybe that was possible—perhaps even reasonable—in an age when virtually all that we knew about science could fit on one shelf in Thomas Jefferson's library. But not today, not in an age when knowledge is increasing and becoming obsolete at a prodigious rate.

I'm not just talking about technology. Geographic boundaries change regularly; history is reinterpreted all the time with discoveries of new information; the mysteries of science yield only to be replaced with new mysteries. For about 75 years, students have been required to memorize the planets, only to learn in 2006 that Pluto is no longer a planet.

Standards and curriculum did not drive the education of many of our founders and early leaders. Many of the people who built this nation and made enduring contributions to society had little or no formal education: George Washington, Abigail Adams, Alexander Hamilton, Patrick Henry, Dolly Madison, Abraham Lincoln, Andrew Johnson, Andrew Jackson, Robert Fulton, Thomas Edison, Herman Melville, Walt Whitman, and millions of ordinary citizens. Once they could read, they acquired the knowledge they needed to be productive workers and good citizens without a core curriculum (or the enormous benefit of the Internet). For those who attended a school, it was customary to leave after the 7th or 8th grade. By and large, our ancestors learned what they needed to learn and wanted to learn, and the more they learned, the more they wanted to learn.

Although elementary schools fail to teach a great many of our children to read well enough to understand what they read, the students are still required in middle school and high school to study (and pass) an array of courses that they lack the skill to master even if, by chance, they are interested in the subject. How reasonable is that?

An early mantra of the school reform movement was that "every student can learn." That is true if it means every student is capable of learning. But that capability can be enhanced or stifled by an inflexible and outdated curriculum. Not all students need to learn the same things in the same way at the same time. And students may be able to learn, but unless they are motivated, they probably won't learn.

Student motivation is probably the most important prerequisite to learning and school success. Standards don't motivate students. Indeed, the philosophy, standardization, and practices of conventional schools do more to stifle motivation than to foster it.

Originally I intended to devote a chapter to the subject of motivation, even though I refer to it throughout this book. I changed my mind when I read Daniel Pink's 2010 best seller, *Drive*.

In it, he challenges the deeply ingrained assumptions that we have about motivation. After I read it, I realized I could not add anything useful to the subject.

| CHAPTER 3 |

If It Moves, Test It

ASSUMPTION: *Standardized test scores provide an accurate measure of student learning and should be used to determine promotion and graduation.*

As some wag said long ago, "If it moves, test it." And we do. The proliferation of standardized testing and its influence on schools and students over the past two decades have even begun to alarm testmakers and psychometricians. The official justification for so much testing is that we need to hold schools and students accountable—the nation needs an accurate picture of how well this important publicly funded institution of public education is performing.

The legitimacy of that argument can be challenged on at least two counts. First, the test scores don't provide an accurate picture for a variety of reasons. Second, even if they did, they would only confirm what is patently obvious: that our conventional schools are not meeting the educational needs of a majority of our students.

No Child Left Behind proclaimed in 2001 that all children would be proficient in reading and math by 2014. That goal was as likely to be met as the one that ensured the presence of a highly qualified teacher in every classroom by 2006 (which is why President Obama abandoned it in March 2010 in his education blueprint for the future).

But then again, perhaps it could have been met depending on how states determined proficiency. The states define proficiency very differently than the National Assessment of Educational

Progress (NAEP), known as the nation's report card. Most states set their passing scores considerably lower than NAEP's. As a result, whereas NAEP generally finds fewer than a quarter of students proficient in reading and math, states, on average, find more than 60 percent proficient; and large districts find that as many as 75 percent of their students are proficient compared to NAEP's finding of only about 25 percent. The gap between NAEP results and those of states and urban districts is huge: from a high of about 50 percentage points in Detroit and Baltimore to 30 percentage points in the District of Columbia and San Diego.

So much for tests providing an accurate picture of school and student performance.

The official response to this disparity is to create common national standards and a new national assessment linked to those standards. Secretary of Education Arne Duncan plans to spend $350 million developing a better assessment. Even if he succeeds and even if states are willing to swallow a bitter pill and accept a new test, the result will not be increased proficiency in reading and math.

If your house is very cold and one thermometer says it is 45 degrees and the other says it is 55 degrees, would your first priority be to find a more accurate thermometer? Clearly, there is something wrong with your heating system, and a more accurate thermometer won't raise the temperature any more than better tests will increase student proficiency.

Discontent with all this testing has been steadily growing. Teachers have become increasingly vocal in their concern about too much standardized testing. According to a recent survey by Public Agenda, 90 percent of U.S. teachers "view the current overemphasis on standardized testing as detrimental to education. . . . Overall, 58% of respondents said too much testing is a major drawback, while 32% said it was a minor drawback" (FairTest, 2009, para. 1).

Teachers claim that they routinely see students who can pass state tests but cannot apply what they "learned" to anything that is not in a test format. In other words, the test becomes an end in itself. Students pass tests but are inept at ordinary school tasks like looking up a word in the dictionary. Most of the teachers in the survey agreed that other measures are better gauges of student learning than tests.

The critics got a boost in 2010, when prominent researcher Diane Ravitch traveled the road to Damascus and saw the light. Ravitch published *The Death and Life of the Great American School System: How Testing and Choice Are Undermining Education*. As a former U.S. assistant secretary of education under the first President Bush, she had ardently promoted standards-based accountability and later No Child Left Behind. Explaining in an op-ed piece in the *Wall Street Journal* why she recanted, Ravitch wrote,

> [A]ccountability turned into a nightmare for American schools, producing graduates who were drilled regularly on the basic skills but were often ignorant about almost everything else. Colleges continued to complain about the poor preparation of entering students, who not only had meager knowledge of the world but still required remediation in basic skills. This was not my vision of good education. (Ravitch, March 9, 2010, para. 9)

Welcome as Ravitch's change of mind is and promising as the Obama administration's view on school reform is in some respects, the undue emphasis on standards and testing continues. Some argue that the $350 million designated to create new assessments aligned with common standards could be better spent to improve schools. Others worry about how a common national curriculum will align with common standards and common assessments. And still others worry about the federal government playing an even greater role in a system that is essentially a state matter. The U.S. Constitution does not mention a federal role for education.

No Child Left Behind was a major step toward greater federal influence. Linking federal funds directly to specific federal goals brought cries of unfunded mandates and even a couple of lawsuits by states (which didn't really go anywhere). NCLB was a boon to the testing industry, resulting in America's schoolchildren taking 56 million standardized reading, math, and science tests a year (Dubner, 2007).

This enormous growth in standardized testing is not based on evidence that such testing is good for schools or students. Quite the contrary, research increasingly warns that it produces significant negative effects on students and learning and should not be relied on to make important educational decisions about schools or students.

Advocates of this testing orgy should at least be challenged to justify and explain its rationale and educational value. Except in school, people are judged by their work and their behavior; few of the business and political leaders who advocate widespread use of standardized testing have taken a standardized test since leaving high school or college. It is probably a safe bet that the majority of them, even after 16 years of formal education, could not pass the tests they require students to pass. "Well," they would protest, "that was a long time ago, and we can't be expected to remember all that stuff we learned."

Exactly! Then why bother "learning" it?

Complicating Factors

Standardized test scores say more about students' cultural background and socioeconomic status than about their abilities. In a study in the late 1980s, Patricia Albjerg Graham, former dean of the Harvard Graduate School of Education, looked closely at early intelligence tests. Because they "appeared" to be scientific, she noted, they reinforced the advice of prominent Harvard president Charles William Eliot, who in 1908 exhorted elementary school teachers to sort their pupils "by their evident or probable destinies." The obvious function of schools, Mr. Eliot was saying, was to shape curriculum to the preconceived notion of children's abilities. The sons and daughters of blue-collar families should receive a different education than the offspring of the professional class.

Here are a couple of sample questions from the U.S. Army test used at the time to evaluate recruits:

Clothing is made by: a) Smith & Wesson; b) Kuppenheimer; c) B. T. Babbitt; d) Swift & Co.

Cambric is a: a) dance; b) fabric; c) food; d) color.

Imagine an immigrant youngster in Boston or an impoverished black kid from the rural South trying to respond to questions like those. For that matter, how many kids from affluent homes know what cambric is?

The correlation between low scores on standardized tests and socioeconomic and cultural background is well established and remains valid today. L. Scott Miller, former officer of the Exxon Education Foundation and author of the award-winning book *An American Imperative: Accelerating Minority Educational Advancement* (1995), found the correlation between SAT scores and students' socioeconomic background so close that colleges could predict students' scores from their background.

Coming at the issue from the cultural side, William J. Mathis, a veteran education administrator in Brandon, Vermont, recently looked at 43 Vermont schools identified on the basis of test scores as not making "adequate yearly progress" under the NCLB law. He asked: What do we know about the communities where the schools are located? And he learned the following:

- The poverty rate is 50 percent higher than the state average.
- The child poverty rate (below 18 years old) is double the state average.
- The child poverty rate (below 5 years of age) is more than double the state average.
- The percentage of households on public assistance is 67 percent higher.
- The percentage with less than a 9th grade education is 35 percent higher.
- The percentage without a high school diploma is 40 percent higher.
- Per capita income is 20 percent lower. (Mathis, 2004)

Researchers at Ohio State University concluded in a 2008 study that as many as three out of four schools deemed to be failing, based on test scores, would be able to meet accountability provisions if they were assessed on measures that are less biased (Grabmeier, 2008). The reason for the disparity is that test scores don't take into account influences beyond the school's control, such as poverty, health issues, and home environment.

Tests that attempt to measure whether schools "add value" to students are increasingly popular in states. Although they are probably an improvement over conventional standardized exit tests, they are still an inadequate measure of school quality.

Stephen W. Raudenbush, Lewis Sebring Distinguished Service Professor in the Department of Sociology at the University of Chicago and chair of the Committee on Education, looked at tests designed to evaluate student proficiency and those developed to measure value added. He had the temerity to deliver a lecture at the Educational Testing Service in Princeton entitled "Schooling, Statistics, and Poverty: Can We Measure School Improvement?" In his address, he asserted that both kinds of tests are inappropriate indicators of school quality because "they are biased against high-poverty schools during the elementary and high school years" (Raudenbush, 2004, p. 4). Dr. Raudenbush added:

> Evidence accumulated over nearly 40 years of educational research indicates that the average level of student outcomes in a given school at a given time is more strongly affected by family background, prior educational experiences out of school, and effects of prior schools than it is affected by the school a student currently attends. (p. 6)

What We *Don't* Test

Quite apart from their obvious biases, standardized tests fail to assess nonacademic traits that parents value and expect their children to get from 12 years in school—such as "people skills," the ability to analyze and evaluate information, to understand the moral implications of their behavior, and, as a Public Agenda poll found, "to be well rounded."

Employers often complain that they have to reteach basic skills to their workers, but when asked what they would like schools to do, they refer to habits of mind and behavior: be punctual, be able to work well with others, be a self-starter—traits not measured by standardized tests. Former student "revolutionary" and now University of Chicago professor Bill Ayers (who became widely known during the 2008 presidential campaign) puts it this way:

> Standardized tests can't measure initiative, creativity, imagination, conceptual thinking, curiosity, effort, irony, judgment, commitment, nuance, good will, ethical reflection, or a host of other valuable dispositions and

attributes. What they can measure and count are isolated skills, specific facts and functions, content knowledge, the least interesting and least significant aspects of learning. (Ayers, 1993, p. 112)

As noted earlier, many teachers bemoan the overuse of tests. They complain that they have no time for many academic or non-academic matters because they are compelled to devote valuable instructional time to preparing students for the tests. They argue that the demands of ubiquitous accountability testing tend to narrow the curriculum. And they say that by teaching to the test, as they are required to do, they must turn education into a game of Trivial Pursuit.

Students are then expected to play the game, and genuine learning is demeaned. Their "work" is reduced to filling in "bubbles" on answer sheets for tests that have no inherent value. Only in their participation out of the classroom—in athletics, theater, music, science fairs, and creative activities like writing and art—are students evaluated on their actual performance. In those activities, students produce something that people can assess on the basis of how well it's done; they demonstrate mastery, skill, and commitment.

Innovative schools tend to use multiple measures to assess student learning and academic performance. They rely on exhibitions, portfolios of work, oral exams and end-of-course tests, internships, and other demonstrations of learning. But state law requires that they also administer the required standardized tests. Only Rhode Island and New Hampshire have revised their graduation requirements to emphasize performance-based assessments and decrease the importance of test scores as credit toward graduation.

The Myth of Objectivity

Advocates of standardized testing argue that scores provide the only objective data available to monitor student progress. Because the tests are scored by machines, they are objective. That also makes them the most efficient way to assess students.

In fact, standardized tests are inevitably subjective because humans, not machines, write and choose the questions. The recent move to include open-ended questions that students must answer in their own words was in response to criticisms of bubble-in answers. But open-ended questions are evaluated by teachers, thereby ensuring that standardized tests are even less objective— and worse, less fair and effective.

Some years ago, I spent a day in Manhattan with half a dozen writers and teachers of writing evaluating the English language arts section of the New York Regents exam, which has long been the "gold standard" in evaluating student proficiency. A new section had recently been added requiring students to read a short excerpt from literature or a factual article or report, then write a short essay reacting to it. The responses had to be graded by human beings—in this case, teachers, not writers, hired for the job.

In the first hour of our discussion, I think there was consensus that it was proper and reasonable to expect any high school senior to meet the writing requirement. As the day wore on and we examined more closely the articles in the test and the students' written responses, we unanimously concluded that the exercise had very little to do with the way people write or should write.

My most vivid memory of that occasion was reading an essay by a student in response to a rather dense and colorless compendium of facts about state parks in New York. His essay was brilliant—a wonderful example of student writing. But then we learned that the teachers grading the exam had given the student a failing grade because he did not include at least two citations and did not follow the format specifications as required.

OK, it's important to follow instructions. But the point of the new writing section was to determine if students could read fairly complex information, understand it, and write a reasonable response to it. This boy did exactly that and was given a failing score for technical mistakes that had little or nothing to do with writing.

The experience reminded me of how often as a student I hesitated over a standardized test question that was written ambiguously or stated in such a way as to seem to be trying to trick me. Even then, I concluded that the testing was more of a game than a genuine effort to determine how well I had learned.

Costs and Consequences

Standardized tests, then, affect education negatively because they are biased and unfair, because they are undependable measures of student ability and learning, and because they divert time and money away from the fundamental mission of schooling: to help students learn to learn and to increase their ability to think and solve problems.

There are conflicting estimates on the cost of standardized testing, but the money diverted isn't small change. Richard Phelps, author of *Defending Standardized Testing* (2005), cites a U.S. Government Accountability Office survey of state and local testing administrators showing the cost to be between $15 and $33 per student.

The National Center for Research on Evaluation, Standards, and Student Testing (CRESST) and the Center for the Study of Testing, Evaluation, and Educational Policy (CSTEEP) estimated in the early 1990s that the cost of state standardized testing ranged from $575 per student to $1,320 (amounts that have undoubtedly risen considerably since then).

Given how little all this testing has improved education, whether the total national cost of systemwide testing is $500 million as the GAO estimates or the $22 billion estimated by the CRESST and CSTEEP, the dollars would have been much better spent on teaching and learning.

As though out-of-control standardized testing weren't negative enough, there is another very important way in which standardized testing undermines education. Virtually every issue of *Education Week* reports on research studies of student performance and achievement. Policymakers and educators use the results of this research to justify important decisions and programs. But because nearly all research on student achievement is based on the flawed metric of standardized test scores, the results of the research are likely to be unreliable. As long as decisions are based on research that assesses student achievement and school performance solely or mainly on standardized test scores, policy and programs are likely to be deeply flawed.

If we really want to know how well students have learned or how successful schools have been in preparing students, we should look at how they fare after school. Longitudinal studies are an effective way to do that, but they are expensive and obviously time consuming.

In 1933, the Progress Education Association launched an eight-year study that has been called "the most important and comprehensive curriculum experiment ever carried out in the United States" (Tanner & Tanner, 1995). The study compared college students who graduated from conventional high schools and whose test scores met the college's admission requirements with graduates of progressive schools for whom admission requirements were waived. The study showed clearly that students from progressive schools significantly outperformed their peers from conventional schools during their college careers. Unfortunately, the study was published in 1942 and was eclipsed by the advent of World War II. It is one of education's most important but least-known stories.

It is hard to argue that standardized tests have no role in accountability. Although students are not required to take it, the National Assessment of Educational Progress has provided a useful snapshot of general educational performance over the years. It is not perfect and it has critics, but NAEP has provided useful data on the effectiveness of the education system as measured by test scores. As long as its limitations are recognized and its influence is proportional, standardized testing at key points along the educational spectrum (such as the 4th, 8th, and 12th grades) can be helpful in gauging the overall state of education.

Unfortunately, those restraints don't now exist. Scores on the states' standardized tests are used to determine whether students are promoted or graduate. Such high-risk tests are now used in about half of the states. How unfair is it to use a single test to decide the future of young people, especially when so many of them did not have the opportunity to learn the material on which they were tested? Policymakers and educational administrators admit that there are mediocre and incompetent teachers in schools, that tests are culturally biased and inadequate indicators of learning, and that they are overused. How, then, can students be penalized for the system's shortcomings?

Standardized test scores should never be used as the basis for policies that affect individual students or schools or for the formulation of important public policy—period.

| CHAPTER 4 |

Make Them Take Algebra

ASSUMPTION: *The United States should require all students to take algebra in the 8th grade and higher-order math in high school largely in order to increase the number of scientists and engineers and thus make us more competitive in the global economy.*

The assumption about algebra and higher-order math has become almost an obsession in policymaking arenas today. Who would disagree that every student should master basic math because it is important in meeting the demands of everyday life? But why should everyone be required to study higher-order math?

The reason most often given is that the United States is not producing enough scientists and engineers to compete in a global economy. Policymakers and business leaders are concerned that students flock to the United States from all over the world to study science and engineering in our universities, then return home to compete with us. More and more of our technical work is being outsourced to countries like India and China. This situation is worrisome because our standard of living and, indeed, our national security are undoubtedly linked to our leadership in science and technology.

To strengthen the quality of the U.S. workforce and gird the American economy against foreign competition, Congress approved "competitive legislation" intended to bolster mathematics and science education by providing federal grants for improved teacher recruitment and training and to promote successful classroom practices. But to assume that the United States will produce more scientists and engineers by requiring every student to take algebra in the 8th grade and higher-order math through high school is like assuming that requiring all high school students to take a few courses in painting will make them artists.

Most students who go to college and major in science and engineering are well on their way before they get to high school. Most become hooked on science or math in the early grades and do well in these subjects in elementary and middle school. They come to experience the delicious satisfaction of solving the mystery, of breaking the code. As they move on to more challenging math studies, they see the beautiful symmetry of mathematics and begin to imagine a career in which math is crucial.

Science provokes endless questions in kids—about the stars, animals, snowflakes, fire, space, and on and on. Gifted teachers can nourish that curiosity and encourage these youngsters to be passionate about science. And that passion may well carry over to a passion for mathematics that will lead some of them to become scientists and engineers. But forcing science on kids is a recipe for failure.

A Recipe for Failure

A 1997 Chicago Public Schools policy increased the number of college-preparatory science courses that students took and passed. But a recent study by the Consortium on Chicago School Research found that the policy also discouraged students from taking higher-level science courses and did not increase the college-going rate. Researchers also found that the increase in the number of science courses taken did not translate into higher grades. Only 15 percent completed three years of science with a *B* average or higher. A coauthor of the report, Nicholas Montgomery, told *Education Week*, "Before the policy, most students received C's and D's in their classes. If they weren't being successful with one or two years of science, why would we think they would be successful with three years of science, if we don't pay attention to getting the students engaged?" (Aarons, 2010b, "Getting C's & D's," para. 5).

Forcing math on students has the same results. Students who reach the 8th grade ready for algebra and higher-order math should be encouraged (not required) to take it, and, I suspect, many of them would. But some won't because they have neither an interest in math nor a talent for it. These students may do well enough to pass their courses, but they are not likely to excel or remember much of what was taught in higher-order mathematics courses. Worse, of course, is the fact that many reach the 8th grade without having learned to read proficiently or do basic arithmetic.

A "Jumble" of Teaching Strategies

Unfortunately, the majority of students do not adequately understand or appreciate mathematics by the time they finish middle school. A report by the National Mathematics Advisory Panel concluded that "the delivery system in mathematics education—the system that translates math knowledge into value and ability for the next generation—is broken and must be fixed" (NMAP, 2008, p. 13). It cites the "jumble" of strategies and theories for teaching math through the elementary grades, and it laments the "math wars," compares them to the "reading wars," and calls them "misguided."

Surely it must be clear that if the nation wants more scientists and engineers, then educators must find some way to agree on what to teach in science and mathematics and how to awaken and nourish a passion for those subjects well before the 8th grade. Even if by some miracle that should occur, it would still be unreasonable to insist that every student take two years of algebra and courses in higher-order math. Some kids will have an avid interest in literature, history, or the arts and may not be interested in math or a career in science. Forcing them into advanced math courses is likely to be counterproductive.

When it was first formulating its math standards, California expected all students (not just those who want to be scientists or engineers) to know that a quadratic equation is one "in which one or more of the terms is squared but raised to no higher power, having the general form $ax^2 + bx + c = 0$, where a, b, and c are constants." Nobel Prize winner Glenn Seaborg pressed hard for that standard, but how many policymakers understand or use such equations? How many now even remember much of what they were taught in higher-order math courses?

Some would argue that is not the point. A main reason for requiring students to study higher-order math is to help them learn to think and solve problems; after all, math is the language of science and engineering. Mathematics is certainly a way of thinking and reasoning for some people and should be available to all students. But for some, philosophy, literature, and history also serve that purpose quite well.

There is no guarantee that simply taking courses in any subject, including higher-order math, will increase a student's thinking skills. *Science Daily* in 2009 reported on a study of 6,000 college freshmen majoring in science and engineering in the United States and China. The study found that Chinese students know more science facts than Americans, but neither group is particularly skilled in scientific reasoning.

No Interest, No Learning

Forcing students to take four years of higher-order math when they have no interest in math and want to be artists or history teachers or journalists is cruel and unusual punishment. Even if a little rubs off, it is probably a waste of time.

Nonetheless, the pressure continues. State graduation requirements in math have steadily increased over the past decade. Twenty-four states now require students to complete three years of math before graduating from high school, according to the Education Commission of the States. Only two states—Alabama and South Carolina—require four years of math, though 10 other states and the District of Columbia are phasing in that requirement (ECS, n.d.).

Requiring more high school math may be counterproductive, according to the findings of the Consortium on Chicago School Research. Its studies revealed that while enrollment in algebra increased, so did the number of students failing math in the 9th grade. At the same time, the researchers say, the change did not seem to produce significant test-score gains for students in math or lead to sizeable increases in the percentages of students who went on to take higher-level math courses later on in high school. *Education Week* reported that "the Chicago school district was at the forefront of that movement in 1997 when it instituted a mandate for 9th grade algebra as part of an overall effort to ensure that its high school students would be 'college ready' upon graduation" (Viadero, 2009, para. 3). Elaine M. Allensworth, the lead researcher on the study, said in an interview that the trend toward more and earlier algebra "seems to be sweeping the country now, and not a lot of thought is being given to how it really affects schools" (para. 6).

More important, how does it affect students? A Brookings Institution study (Loveless, 2008) offers some answers. *The Misplaced Math Student: Lost in Eighth Grade Algebra* finds that many of the lowest-performing students required to take 8th grade algebra are as far as six grades below grade level in math. Tom Loveless, one of the researchers, argues that efforts to require all students to take introductory algebra, or Algebra 1, in 8th grade are well meaning but ultimately misguided. Policymakers would be better off, he advises, to concentrate on grounding elementary students in the math they need for algebra and intervening with the ones who need extra help. Mr. Loveless told *Education Week* that the issue is even more complex because "no one has figured out how to teach algebra to kids who are seven or eight years behind before they get to algebra, and teach it all in one year" (Viadero, 2010, "Basic Arithmetic," para. 2).

Nonetheless, the number of 8th graders nationally taking algebra has nearly doubled to 31 percent since 1990. Many of the states with the highest percentages of students enrolled in 8th grade algebra had the lowest average math scores in that grade on the 2007 NAEP. California, for example, enrolls almost 60 percent of its 8th graders in Algebra 1 or another advanced math course but has one of the nation's lowest average scores on NAEP (Cavanagh, 2008). Perhaps that explains why a Sacramento County superior court judge in 2008 issued a temporary restraining order blocking the new mandate that California students be required to take algebra in the 8th grade.

Advocates argue fiercely that to exempt some students from higher-order math is a form of invidious tracking because it would likely prevent them from doing many jobs in the modern workforce. They rightly point out that higher-order math is not only a college admission requirement but also a prerequisite to fully understanding and "doing the work" of science and engineering.

What Do Employers Want?

Labor experts, however, say the skills that employers—even those in many high-paying fields—demand don't include the high-level math that policymakers are pushing for. Employers say that fluency in advanced math topics is less crucial than skill in problem solving and in applying math to different tasks. And they contend that creating courses that place a greater emphasis on real-world or "applied" math, as opposed to simply increasing academic requirements, could improve not only students' workforce skills but also their enthusiasm for that subject. In a survey of 51 employers, 35 said they required workers to know relatively basic math, such as how to do simple arithmetic and to add fractions, although some jobs required algebra and trigonometry; but some managers said they had difficulty finding workers with even basic math skills (Cavanagh, 2007).

Michael J. Handel, a professor of sociology at Northeastern University in Boston, surveyed 2,300 employees from a broad range of job backgrounds, including "upper-white-collar" workers, such as managers and technicians; "lower-white-collar" employees, such as salespeople; and a range of blue-collar and service employees, such as factory and food-service workers. Handel found that although 94 percent of workers across those occupations reported using some kind of math on the job, just 22 percent said they used any math more advanced than adding, subtracting, multiplying, or dividing. Only 19 percent said they used skills taught in Algebra 1, and 9 percent used Algebra 2. Most workers said they used more basic math, such as fractions, multiplication, and division. Only 14 percent of higher-level employees, such as managers, said they used Algebra 2 in their work (Cavanagh, 2007).

Stanley Goldstein, founder of the CVS pharmacy chain, once told me, "I have been a successful businessman for 40 years; I founded and ran a Fortune 500 company, and the only math I ever used was addition, subtraction, division, multiplication, and figuring percentages in my head."

If public schools worked as they should, every student would be proficient in math by the 8th grade and many would eagerly study algebra, geometry, trigonometry, and calculus. But if schools don't prepare young people in their first eight years for such courses, how in good conscience can we require them to take four years of higher-order math in high school?

CHAPTER 5

Wanted: Great Teachers

ASSUMPTION: *We need to put a highly qualified teacher in every class-room to deliver an excellent education to every student and improve our schools.*

The assumption about highly qualified teachers is the conventional wisdom—and it isn't hard to believe. Nearly all of us can remember at least one wonderful teacher who had a positive effect on our lives.

I had several, but one was truly influential. As a senior about to graduate from Munhall High School near Pittsburgh, Pennsylvania, I expected to work in the steel mills like most of my peers. On the last day of classes, my favorite teacher (she taught English) ended the class by asking those planning to attend college to raise their hands. Only about 5 out of 30 students did, and I was not one of them. As the bell rang, she pointed to me and said, "Wait. We need to talk."

She asked why I wasn't going to college. I shrugged and told her that I wanted to go but didn't have the money. Before I left her room, she and I had filled out my application to Westminster College in New Wilmington, Pennsylvania, and she assured me that I would get the aid I needed to attend. She changed my life! If it hadn't been for her, I'd probably be a retired steelworker in Munhall.

Plenty of books and movies extol the dedicated teacher who defies all the odds and breaks through the barriers of distrust and disinterest to light the lamp of learning for her students. There are examples of defiant, unruly students who run wild in one classroom and become docile and engaged in the next classroom—mainly because of the teacher. Good teachers challenge their students, inspire them, nourish their curiosity, and demonstrate over and over again that teaching is an act of love.

I would not even try to dispute the assumption that putting a highly qualified teacher in every classroom would increase student learning and educational success. It isn't wrong, it's just not possible. It makes no sense to formulate a school improvement strategy and set unrealistic goals on a premise that is not sound. The goal is unreachable because it is a statistical impossibility to guarantee that every one of the nation's 3 million teachers will be an excellent teacher. As in any endeavor this big, individuals will be distributed across a spectrum of quality—from a relative handful who are so bad they shouldn't be teaching to a relative handful who are outstanding. The great majority fall somewhere in between.

Just as all of us have had good teachers, we have also had mediocre ones and even bad ones. A rational system would acknowledge this and then redesign itself to optimize the positive influence of good teachers, minimize the negatives of less good teachers, and continually work to improve teachers in between.

Instead, President George W. Bush and Congress passed No Child Left Behind in 2001, mandating that there would be a highly qualified teacher in every classroom by 2006. Not surprisingly, the goal was not met and four years later remains unmet, even though the law defines "highly qualified" as a teacher who is certified by a state. State certification guarantees high quality about as much as a driver's license guarantees a good driver. What is confounding—even a bit scary—about this mandate is that the architects and supporters of No Child Left Behind seemed honestly to believe it would be possible to staff every classroom with a highly qualified teacher in six years.

Three Barriers to Great Teaching

If we adopted better policies and took effective actions, we might at least have a chance of increasing the number of good teachers, reducing the number of bad teachers, and improving the skills and knowledge of more of those who fall in between. I say "might have a chance" because there are three barriers to achieving this goal that have proved virtually insurmountable:

- Removing incompetent teachers from the classroom
- Attracting a sufficient number of the "best and brightest" students into the teaching profession
- Reforming the way teachers are prepared for the very demanding role they play

Unless these goals can be accomplished, the chances of significantly improving and retaining the teacher corps the nation needs are nil. This whole book could be devoted to those three issues, but I will discuss them only briefly, beginning with the problem of removing incompetent teachers.

In its August 31, 2009 issue, *The New Yorker* published a devastating article called "The Rubber Room" by Steven Brill. It opens with a cartoon, and the caption reads: "One school principal has said that Randi Weingarten, of the teachers' union, 'would protect a dead body in the classroom.'"

The picture Brill paints is almost surreal. And the stories he tells of various "rubber room" occupants are so bizarre they are hard to believe and even harder to tolerate.

The "rubber room" is a "temporary reassignment center" (one of a number of such places) where some 600 of New York City's worst teachers are sent to get them out of the classroom. Although some have been accused of child molesting, misconduct, violence against children, and simple incompetence, they while away their days in the "rubber room" sleeping, reading, playing games, or doing nothing while receiving full pay and benefits. They spend an average of three years in the rubber room, according to Brill, while the school district and the union and their lawyers wrangle over efforts to dismiss them.

The Dance of the Lemons

Union contracts across the country so fiercely protect teachers that firing an incompetent teacher can take years and be very expensive. Ironically, the same union contract also largely dictates who principals must hire to staff the schools. Contracts give teachers "bumping rights." Senior teachers have their pick of job openings, and new teachers cannot be hired until the more senior teachers choose. Principals must hire teachers from within the district on the basis of teacher preference and seniority. Teachers who transfer from other schools—even though some may be transferring because of poor performance—have to be hired in the school of their choice at the expense of a less experienced teacher. This is known as "the dance of the lemons."

Administrators and policymakers have been complaining about the problem for years but have been unable to solve it. But in 2009, Rhode Island school chief Peter McWalters ordered the Providence school superintendent to override the union contract bumping provision. Hiring authority should move from the districts to the school level, McWalters asserted, and teachers should be hired on the basis of student need and teacher effectiveness rather than preference or seniority. Principals could interview teachers who wanted to work in their schools and would have the final say about whom they accepted in their schools. McWalters kicked over a hornet's nest, and the issue was in the courts at the time of this writing.

The hiring and firing of teachers is one of the most contentious issues in education—and one of the most important because it involves evaluation, tenure, accountability, due process, and ultimately the quality of education. A study by the New Teacher Project (Levin, Mulhern, & Schunck, 2005) documented the negative effects of "bumping rights" and tenure. The study found that in five major city school districts, 40 percent of school-level vacancies, on average, were filled by teachers who decided to transfer or were "excessed," that is, had lost their jobs as a result of schools downsizing and closing. Schools had either no choice at all or limited choice in hiring staff. One principal decried the process as "not about the best-qualified [teacher] candidate but rather satisfying union rules" (p. 10).

Even when hiring policies are changed to permit hiring decisions not based solely on seniority, the districts can lose. A recent New Teacher Project report (Daley et al., 2008) noted that excessed teachers are placed in a "reserve pool and have to apply for new jobs," but they receive full salaries and benefits while waiting for a new job. In New York City, the cost in one year was $81 million in salary and benefits to excessed teachers who had not found new full-time positions by the end of the 2007 school year.

The seniority provisions make principals hesitant to announce job openings, hoping the senior "lemons" will all have chosen a job by the time the opening is posted. Of course, the delay often results in the loss of the new teacher applicants anyway, as confirmed by another study by the New Teacher Project (Levin & Quinn, 2003). The study looked at hiring in large urban school districts and found that "strategic recruitment brought hundreds of applicants, but 31–58% of them withdrew; 50–70% of withdrawers cited late hiring timelines as a major reason they found other jobs" (p. 4). The negative effect on schools is significant. The New Teacher Project study notes that the teacher applicants who withdrew had higher college grades and "were 40 percent more likely to have a degree in their teaching field, and were significantly more likely to have completed educational coursework" than the teachers who ended up staying around to finally receive job offers (p. 6).

Over several years, I watched this scenario play out in Providence with one of the district's best high schools. The district-created charter school operates under the union contract and has lost principals and bright, eager teachers because it was forced to hire teachers who do not share the school's philosophy or goals. The morale of teachers, parents, and students has declined, along with the quality of the education.

A Problem of Supply

The second daunting barrier to improving the nation's teacher corps is a supply problem: How can enough bright, committed young people be attracted to the profession? The "bumping" provision of union contracts and the consequent long delays in hiring new teachers are only part of the problem.

Even after they get hired, as many as half of the people who enter the field leave within five years. In various surveys, more than half of the teachers polled cited such factors as working conditions, bureaucracy, lack of support in the classroom, and poor staff morale as reasons they left the profession (National Center for Education Statistics, 2000–01). Of these, working conditions probably ranks as the most serious problem.

Although we refer to teaching as a profession, not much about the job is professional. Professionals like doctors and lawyers set their own performance standards, hold their members accountable for meeting those standards, determine to a large degree (or at least significantly influence) their own working conditions, and receive compensation perceived to be commensurate with their professional contributions to society.

Teachers, by contrast, have little to say about their working conditions except for the work rules in their union contracts. They don't decide what students should be taught or the nature of the curriculum, have almost no influence on educational policy, and play almost no role in setting performance standards for teachers or evaluating their performance. Even if they did, contract restrictions would ensure that the reviews would have little consequence, either positive or negative. Unions don't like to make any kind of distinctions among teachers.

Compare the teacher workplace with that of other professionals. Instead of having offices and secretaries, teachers are isolated in classrooms where they have little contact with their fellow teachers. Their work schedule is decided for them, and it is a long-standing complaint that they have trouble finding time to use the lavatory, let alone share a cup of coffee with a colleague.

Teachers have little opportunity to collaborate and work in teams and thus to learn from each other. The MetLife Survey of the American Teacher (Harris Interactive, 2009) found that 69 percent of teachers believe their voices aren't heard in the debate on education. Although nearly all teachers say they participate in some collaborative activity, 67 percent of them and 78 percent of principals believe that student achievement would be significantly increased by more collaboration. In short, almost nothing in schools enhances teachers' personal growth or their influence on policy.

Even as I write that, I recall a visit to a high school in East Cleveland where the teachers were poised to vote on a major reform proposal that they had crafted during more than a year of discussion. Local foundations had funded the effort, and a committee of teachers had been able to participate in extended meetings in accommodations usually reserved for big shots.

The plan was killed by a vote of the teachers. I recall asking the chairwoman to explain how the faculty could vote no on a plan that their peers had spent more than a year formulating. Her answer stunned me and forever changed my perspective. "Teachers don't become teachers because they want to change schools," she said. "They liked school; they liked their classes and their teachers. That's why they became teachers."

"Professional development" is one of those "blah-blah" terms that is shorthand for continuous learning to enrich one's knowledge and improve one's craft. Traditionally, it comprises the college courses teachers take in the evening or the summer to move up on the salary scale and the "hit-and-run" workshops that schools hold once or twice a year in which outside experts tell teachers how to be better teachers. This kind of professional development does little, if anything, to improve teaching and student learning.

In recent years, opportunities have increased for teachers to participate in substantive professional development programs that they help plan. A number of studies have shown that this more sophisticated professional development is apt to help teachers improve. But for most teachers, that goal remains largely unmet.

According to a 1995 policy brief by the Consortium for Policy Research in Education, "most states and districts have no idea of what they are actually spending on professional development. They cannot even estimate overall expenditures because the data needed are not available. State accounting systems make it difficult to aggregate professional development expenditures and few districts attempt to track them." Growing attention to teacher professional development may be at least moving states in the direction of more clarity and coherence. There is some progress in getting policymakers to stop thinking of professional development as a boondoggle or a fringe benefit.

Salary is another element in the conversation. Teachers are responsible for educating our children—a service to society at least as important as that of any profession—but they do not earn comparable salaries.

Even though there is no evidence that compensation is a major reason why teachers enter or leave the profession, the first impulse of policymakers has been to consider higher salaries as the best way to attract and retain good teachers. Teaching is not compensated as well as many other white-collar occupations, but teacher unions have generally negotiated better than average benefits and reasonable salaries for experienced teachers for a 180-day work year. Since their work is linked to the school year, teachers tend to get most of the summer off. They also spend about seven hours a day on average in school—leading to complaints that teachers work "bankers' hours."

A case can be made for higher starting salaries as a long-term strategy to attract more bright and committed college students into teaching. But to simply raise salaries across the board on the assumption that this will improve teaching is comparable to assuming that if we pay pilots more, flying will be safer.

There are plenty of examples of teachers who operate on autopilot, but despite the short work day and work year, committed teachers put much more time into their work than most people realize.

When I was planning to launch *Teacher Magazine* in the late 1980s (as the "first professional magazine that wouldn't treat teachers as tall children"), I interviewed scores of teachers across the country. The most memorable interview was with a teacher who was being honored at a national conference. I described what I had in mind and asked for her opinion. "Sounds great," she replied enthusiastically. "The articles you describe are right on and very relevant."

"Would you subscribe?" I asked.

"Oh no," she said, "I wouldn't have time to read a magazine like that."

"You're supposed to be a professional," I scolded. "How can you not do what you need to do to keep up with developments in your profession and the issues that are shaping what you do in the classroom?"

Her tone sharpened as she responded: "Listen, mister, I get up every morning at 5:30 to get my three kids off to school; to fix their breakfast and make sure they have their books and homework and get to the bus stop on time. I get to school no later than 7:30 so I can plan and organize my day and review my lesson plans. I check my notes about students who are struggling. I go from one class to another, serve regularly as a hall monitor, oversee the kids at lunch when it's my turn, and attend to the crappy little stuff that we all have to deal with."

Before I could interrupt, she continued: "I rarely leave school before 4 p.m. because I've got paperwork and things I must do to be ready for the next day. When I get home, I have to get started on dinner, make sure my kids are doing their homework, chauffeur one or another of them to some event. By 6:30 or 7, I have a few minutes to talk with my husband and watch the news. Then I've got a couple of hours of work to correct papers and work on my lesson plans for the next day. I fall into bed by 10 totally exhausted." She paused and then said, "If you think I am going to spend a couple of hours reading a magazine about teaching, you're crazy."

I learned painfully that her view was widely shared. Despite having sent marketing letters to at least 3 million teachers, our magazine—cited twice by the National Magazine Association for quality—never had more than about 40,000 paid subscribers.

How strange and ironic it is that teachers, whose profession is to disseminate knowledge, have so little time and opportunity to acquire it.

Part of the reason is that teachers (and principals) lead their work lives in real time, constantly engaged in the moment. They may not actually be busier than a lawyer or an accountant, but they feel they are because they have almost no control over their time. Their days are strictly scheduled; they are prisoners of an inflexible curriculum; they have little interaction with fellow workers; they have no time for reflection or anticipation; they have almost no say in how their schools are organized or run.

How can anyone believe that the goal of placing a "good" teacher in every classroom can be achieved without changing the conditions in which teachers work—the way schools are structured and operated?

Not only does the present structure hide and shelter incompetence, it undermines good teaching and discourages teachers' professional growth. It is unfair to good teachers and to the many who are less competent but capable of getting better.

Preparing Teachers for Yesterday

The third major barrier to putting a highly qualified teacher in every classroom—and perhaps the most important—is the way colleges and universities prepare the vast majority of teachers for their work.

Over the past quarter-century, dozens of professional organizations and research groups have conducted studies of how teachers are prepared. Taken together, they have described a badly broken system, out of date and incompatible with the challenges facing today's teachers.

In the mid-1980s, a group of education school deans formed the Holmes Group to reform teacher education. By 1995 the Holmes Group had become a network of more than 80 universities, and it was still calling for "an overhaul" of schools of education.

In a 116-page report, *Tomorrow's Schools of Education*, the group said education schools in the leading research universities in the United States needed to thoroughly overhaul their programs or "surrender their franchise." The report warned that schools of education "should cease to act as a silent agent in the preservation of the status quo" (Bradley, 1995, para. 1–2).

The oft-cited criticisms of teacher preparation programs became headlines again a few years ago in a multivolume study by Arthur Levine, former president of Teachers College, Columbia University. In the report *Educating School Teachers*, Levine (2006) asserted that most of our teachers are trained in university teacher preparation programs that have low standards, unimpressive faculty, and out-of-date courses. A *Wall Street Journal* article (2006) describing the report notes that "three-quarters of the country's 1,206 university-level schools of education don't have the capacity to produce excellent teachers" (para. 1).

A 2009 report by the National Council on Teacher Quality agreed and focused on a specific failure: ". . . preparing aspiring elementary teachers for what is often characterized as their most important task: teaching children to read." The report said that almost all of the 72 institutions in the sample studied "earned a 'failing' grade" (Manzo, 2006, para. 1, 3).

The late Al Shanker, founder of the American Federation of Teachers, would not be surprised by these findings. He used to say that so many of our kids are not good readers because many of their teachers are not good readers. He noted that teachers usually take only one course in reading instruction in college.

For several decades critics have railed against colleges and universities for low standards, gut courses, and lack of rigor in their teacher preparation programs. Linda Darling-Hammond, professor of education at Stanford, says: "Too many universities still offer fragmented coursework and haphazard clinical placements, disconnected from one another" (Darling-Hammond, Haselkorn, & Bouw, 2009, para. 3).

Critics charge that schools of education prepare teachers to teach subjects rather than students. Prospective teachers have a bare minimum of exposure to clinical practice during their preparation and rarely have an inkling of the human problems they will face when they enter their classroom. A telling example comes from John Merrow, producer of *Learning Matters*, who made a video of education students pretending to be 8th graders so their fellow students could get an idea of what it's like to work with teenage students. A lot of actual 8th graders were in class in a public middle school just a few blocks away.

The many critical reports of teacher education with their many recommendations to lift the profession have attracted media attention but have not moved higher education to reform teacher preparation programs. Except for a few institutions that prove the rule, like Alvorno College in Wisconsin, which is a lonely "poster child" for good teacher education, most teacher education programs are still preparing students for schools as they were nearly a century ago.

College presidents would never tolerate mediocrity in their medical or law schools, but they knowingly look the other way when it comes to teacher preparation programs. How can they not see the irony in demanding higher quality in their student applicants while simultaneously accepting lower-quality education for their teachers? How do they fail to see that it is in their own interest to do everything possible to ensure that the high school students they admit are well prepared so they don't need remedial courses? Or is it that they don't want to mess with what are commonly known to be "cash cows" for the institution?

We could go a long way toward staffing our schools with highly qualified teachers without great expenditure of funds if we adopted the key recommendations that so many reports have laid out after careful and thorough study. That would mean, of course, dramatically changing the way teacher preparation programs and public schools have been run for more than a century. Until such changes are made and until teachers are prepared and treated like true professionals, we cannot reasonably expect to get the teachers our students need and deserve.

A Challenge for Teacher Unions

Finally, a word about teacher unions. It is widely believed by policymakers, opinion leaders, and the public that unions are the biggest obstacle to school improvement. There is no doubt that when unions must choose between what is best for their members and what may be best for their students, they do what unions were created to do—look out for their members. But if the unions have become too powerful, the administrators and policymakers are largely to blame.

The American Federation of Teachers and the National Education Association have about 3.2 million active teacher members. Both have gained members during the last few decades and now have extraordinary power. They are well represented in many state legislatures and have increased their influence through contributions to election campaigns of their political allies, which increases their influence on education legislation and policy.

Until relatively recently, school boards and superintendents have been no match for the teacher unions in negotiations, and over the years teacher contracts have become ever more favorable to teachers. The hiring and firing provisions mentioned earlier are only one of the ways the unions have shaped education. They have won work rules that restrict districts in changing schedules and curricula; they have even sued districts to stop them from combining two academic departments. Unions have fought for and won compensation packages that include pension and health care benefits that are much better than those many other working citizens enjoy. And they have managed to thwart or greatly modify a number of reforms, like teacher evaluation, length of school day and year, charter schools and vouchers, and alternative routes to teaching.

In recent years, districts have begun bringing their own labor lawyers to the bargaining table and have become more adept in the negotiations. The result has been more media coverage generally unfavorable to unions and fractured relations between teachers and other parts of the community. In the ongoing battle between the adults in the system, the students suffer.

Here's an example. Halfway through the 2009–10 school year, the superintendent of the school district in Central Falls, Rhode Island, was instructed by the state schools chief to "fix" the failing local high school that had been declared persistently low performing. Under a recent federal decision to tie school improvement to federal grants, the superintendent had to choose one of four options: (1) close the school, (2) turn it over to a charter-management organization, (3) transform it, or (4) fire the entire staff and start over. The superintendent chose the transformation model and proposed a plan that would require teachers to work an extra half hour a day, participate in a professional development program during the summer, and tutor and spend more time with students.

Because the plan involved teacher pay and time, it was a negotiable issue under the union contract. Although teachers would receive an additional $3,400 per year for their extra time, the negotiations broke down. As reported in the *Providence Journal*, one union official stated, "This is not about time and money; it's about our right to negotiate time and money" (Jordan, 2010, para. 39).

Unable to persuade the union to accept the plan, the superintendent then chose the turnaround option requiring her to fire the principal and all the teachers. The brouhaha made national news and was mentioned by both President Obama in a speech and by Secretary of Education Arne Duncan. At this writing, the district and the union have reached a fragile compromise.

In one form or another, the Central Falls battle is fought across the nation every year. As the opening day of school approaches, teachers in many districts strike or threaten to strike if their demands are not met.

In a way, it is disingenuous to fault a labor union for doing well what it is designed to do. The unions gained their power by influencing policy and outmaneuvering district superintendents and school boards over the years.

That they might be a bit skeptical about the promise of various reforms proposed is understandable. And there is little reason to think that education officials or policymakers will get it right; in fact, their past record suggests otherwise.

Moreover, the government giveth and the government may taketh away. States have the authority to curb the power of unions. And if too many legislators are "owned" by the unions, then the public has the authority to replace the legislators.

The unions need to acknowledge that their influence has become so great that the balance of power has been upset, and they must be willing to negotiate contracts that are much more sympathetic to the needs of students. The states and districts need to acknowledge that teachers should have a significant say in how schools are run as well as in regard to their own benefits.

It is time to restore the balance for the benefit of both the kids and the society.

CHAPTER 6

The Quest for the Supreme Leader

ASSUMPTION: *Having an effective principal in every school would make the difference between a school that works and one that doesn't.*

In my early days at *Education Week* I attended a conference to hear Ron Edmonds give the keynote address. He was the founder of the Effective Schools movement that was just getting under way, and I wanted to meet him.

At one of the sessions at that meeting, a principal told of how he had turned around a failing New York City high school. For the first few months he studied the school to figure out why discipline was such a problem, attendance was so low, dropout rates were so high, and neither the students nor the faculty were much engaged in learning. He then assembled the students and staff to explain what he planned to do. It was something of a pep talk, he said. And when he finished, he told the gathering in an oratorical flourish: "We can do this. We can turn this school around if we work together. Are you with me?"

Well, he told us, the crowd responded with a loud: "Noooooooo!"

Chagrined but not deterred, he pushed ahead in his effort to link academics to career options. He persuaded a retired United Airlines pilot to give a course in navigation. About 20 students were enrolled, and they had to learn some math, some meteorology, some physics, and some aerodynamics. And they had to learn to speak formal English so they could communicate with the control towers and other pilots. The pilot promised that every student who had no unexcused absences would get a chance to fly with him in his own plane. As I recall, 17 of the 20 made it. Many of them had never been out of New York City.

This bold and creative principal worked with a local hospital to give a course in different aspects of health care, a restaurant manager to give a course in food services, and so on. Attendance rates and grades went up, and dropout rates declined. After five years, his plan was working. Then, in a dispute with the central office, the principal left. Within a year the high school had reverted to the state it was in when he began.

Caught in the Middle

Over a period of time, I discovered that the story held a number of lessons: resistance to change, the courage to lead, the importance of relevance, and others. I also learned the importance of sharing leadership. Principals who empower their teachers and students by persuading them to participate in planning and decision making will be more likely to succeed. But the sad and perhaps most important lesson was that isolated, idiosyncratic change in a system is fragile and often disappears when the charismatic leader leaves. That is a lesson I saw repeated many times over the years at all levels—classroom, school, district, and state.

Principals can indeed play a critical role in making a school more successful, but that success is likely to be ephemeral if the larger system does not change to embrace and protect it.

I spent a day at the Baltimore City College High School. Founded in 1839 as a "test" school (one that admits students by test scores), City College admitted only the brightest white boys in Baltimore. Morale and standards were high. Teachers were devoted and revered. The walls of this Oxford-like building were adorned with portraits of distinguished alumni who were leaders in many walks of life.

After *Brown v. Board* in 1954, the school admitted black boys, and in the late 1960s it began admitting girls. At least a quarter of these new students were admitted not on the basis of test scores but by references, interviews, and grades.

Despite these substantial changes, morale, standards, teaching, grades, and school spirit did not decline. The culture of excellence that had been built for 115 years through the terms of many principals sustained the school as it adapted to the changes and challenges of an uncertain future. The success of City College was not due to effective principals, but to that enduring culture of excellence.

To base policy or action on the assumption that an effective principal is the answer to failing and mediocre schools is unreasonable even though the odds of being able to put an effective principal in every school are much better than the odds of putting a high-quality teacher in every classroom. There are about 100,000 public schools in the United States, so there are probably about 100,000 principals (Center for Education Reform, 2009b). That is obviously a more manageable number than 3.2 million. And the teacher workforce provides a defined and easily reached labor pool for principals. Still, the odds are long.

Systemic changes will be required to ensure that even most schools have an effective principal. The following are some of the issues that need to be addressed:

- Principals' effectiveness is determined largely by the programs that prepare them, the authority they have to carry out their responsibilities, and the conditions they work under.
- The archaic organization of schools and the enormous challenges they face make it extremely difficult, if not impossible, for a principal to be effective, although the chances are better at the elementary school level and in smaller schools.
- The many demands on principals are daunting. They are expected to be the CEO, a skilled organizational manager, a strong instructional leader, a strategic planner, an inspirational figure, a politician, and a community relations expert.
- Limits restrain the power of principals to be innovative and decisive. In fact, they are more like sergeants in an army—caught in the middle between the higher-ranking administrators above and the teachers (and students and parents) below.

These are formidable obstacles. As noted in Chapter 5, principals lack the authority to hire or dismiss their teachers. Their hands are often tied by teacher union contracts that govern major aspects of school operation. The central office allocates the schools' funds and generally sets the educational and administrative agenda.

Like a Battlefield Commander

Anyone who shadows the principal of a large urban high school for a day soon discovers that the "principal instructional leader" (like teachers) lives in real time, with little opportunity for planning or reflection and almost no time for instruction or collaboration with colleagues. In large schools, the principal, often with a squawking walkie-talkie in hand, patrols the halls herding students to class, peering into classrooms, and handling a variety of crises. As with teachers, universities' preparation programs do not prepare principals for the real world of schools and are often irrelevant to the reality the principal will face.

Some years ago, under the auspices of the Klingenstein Institute of Teachers College, I spent most of a day "shadowing" the principal of Brooklyn Technical High School, a school that specializes in math, science, and engineering. Like Baltimore City College High School, mentioned earlier, Brooklyn Tech is a "test" school, and it has been cited as one of the best magnet schools in the country (Educational Networks, n.d.).

The principal, a six-foot-four-inch African American man, invited me to accompany him on his morning walk through the massive building. The school, which occupies a city block, was built to house about 6,000 students but enrolled only half that when I visited. Even so, the place was bustling with kids, most of them minorities who represented a number of races and nationalities. As I stood at an intersection of hallways with the principal and looked into the faces of the rushing students, I realized I was seeing the future of America.

It was important, the principal told me, that he be seen—and he was very visible as rivers of students rushed around him. I noted that the kids were all wearing their winter coats and hats, and he explained that it was because the kids didn't want them to be stolen.

What I remember most about the day was that the principal went from one crisis to another—fights in the hallways, a spat between a couple breaking up, a meeting with a union rep and a teacher the principal had spent many weeks trying to fire. I felt like I was following a general in a war zone.

At the end of the day, he prepared to stand outside the school doors and watch his students leave to make sure they dispersed without getting into trouble with each other or hangers-on across the street. As we were leaving his office, a secretary pointed to a young man who had the forms necessary to transfer out of a class. In his one instructional task of the day, the principal studied the form, and then something like the following dialogue took place:

> *Principal:* You want to transfer because you are not interested in the course?
> *Student:* Yes.
> *Principal:* Did you pass history last semester?
> *Student:* No.
> *Principal:* Did you pass algebra?
> *Student:* No.
> *Principal:* Did you pass English?
> *Student:* [hesitates] I don't remember.

I was stunned by that answer. The principal shook his head, signed the form, and we left. Obviously, this incident doesn't define the high school, but it certainly left a troubling impression.

Outdated Principal Preparation

The preparation of principals is as deficient as the preparation of teachers. In a Public Agenda survey several years ago, an incredible 80 percent of superintendents and 69 percent of principals said that leadership training in schools of education is "out of touch with the realities of what it takes to run today's schools" (Finn, 2002, para. 7). According to a study by the Institute for Educational Leadership, "Neither organized professional development programs nor formal preparation programs based in higher education institutions have adequately prepared those holding these jobs to meet the priority demands of the 21st century" (Hale & Moorman, 2003, "Introduction," para. 5). The report adds that "the general consensus in most quarters is that principal preparation programs (with a few notable exceptions) are too theoretical and totally unrelated to the daily demands on contemporary principals" (Hale & Moorman, 2003, "What Is the Current Condition," para. 5). One prominent leader in the movement to improve principal preparation has described it as "bankrupt," and another concedes that "university programs have been slow to change and that faculties are not connected to the field" (para. 3).

As in the preparation of teachers, aspiring principals have too little clinical experience. Most principals are former teachers, but few of them have a genuine understanding of the principal's job.

The Wallace Foundation has funded successful programs that permit an aspiring principal to work as an apprentice to a veteran principal for a year (Archer, 2004). The Broad Foundation and other foundations have funded similar programs to improve administrative leadership. And the federal Department of Education planned to spend nearly $30 million in 2010 on principal training, which the head of the National Association of Secondary Schools called "a drop in the bucket" (Aarons, 2010a, para. 4).

Training principals is essential but not sufficient for effective school leadership. Their working conditions must also be improved, and they must have authority commensurate with their responsibility. Education leaders and state policymakers must address these challenges as well. If every public school were led by a strong and dedicated principal, some progress would surely result. But without major changes in all other aspects of the conventional school, the principal's influence for positive change will be severely limited.

CHAPTER 7

The Dropout Epidemic

ASSUMPTION: *The student dropout rate can be reduced by dropout-prevention programs and raising the mandatory attendance age from 16 to 18.*

Arguably, the student dropout rate is the most damning evidence of the nation's educational failure. The cost in human and financial terms is staggering.

Every school day, some 7,000 youngsters drop out of school; that is almost 1.2 million annually. About one in three students who enter the 9th grade leave school without graduating (LoMonaco, 2008).

The problem is far worse in urban districts and among poor minority students. More than 600,000 dropouts from the Class of 2008—roughly half the number annually—attended school districts in and around 50 major cities (Alliance for Excellent Education, 2010). In many urban districts the dropout rate exceeds 50 percent; in Detroit, it is a horrendous 75 percent (Fields, 2008). A Johns Hopkins University study of dropouts (Balfanz & Legters, 2004) indicted some 2,000 high schools as "dropout factories." They are located in nearly every state, but are concentrated in northern and some western cities, southern and southwestern states, and three mega-districts—New York City, Chicago, and Los Angeles.

In general, dropouts are more likely to be condemned to a lower standard of living and an unpromising future. They are disproportionately unemployed or underemployed. They are more likely to be in the criminal justice system. Because they will earn far less than peers with more education, they will tend to rely much more on governmental services like health care, housing, welfare, and food stamps. Various studies show that the financial cost to society of the dropout problem is enormous. The human cost is incalculable. Moreover, the problem tends to be generational. The children of adults whose own education was deficient are more likely to be unready for school, less proficient academically, and more likely to find themselves on the path to dropping out.

The High Cost to Society

An analysis by the Alliance for Excellent Education (2010) shows that the U.S. economy would grow significantly if the number of high school dropouts were cut in half. If just half of these students had graduated, research shows, they would have generated more than $4.1 billion in additional earning every year, and states and localities would have received additional taxes of more than $535 million. If the nation continues to lose students at the present rate, about 13 million students will drop out in the next 10 years at a financial loss of $3 trillion (Alliance for Excellent Education, 2009).

Obviously, saving money by reducing the dropout rate is a worthwhile goal. But our main reason for action should be to rescue millions of kids from a bleak future.

There is even a question in my mind about whether the projected savings are real.

I've seen various estimates of the cost of the dropout problem, but I've never seen an analysis of the costs of solving it. I'm no economist, but we know that it costs money to keep kids in school. The average per-pupil expenditure nationally totals about $10,000 in combined state and local allocations annually and is higher in many of the largest urban districts.

It follows logically that if we cut the dropout rate in half—keeping 600,000 more students in school each year—states and localities would have to come up with an additional $600 million—more than the estimated $535 million in estimated new state and local tax revenues. Moreover, the burden of the increased costs would fall largely on the urban districts that need more resources to fulfill their educational mission.

The financial costs of the dropout problem are in foregone income and less tax revenue, so the effect is spread across various social services and economic sectors. It is difficult to feel the pain of losing something you never had. But the cost of reducing the dropout rate and keeping more kids in school would be felt almost immediately and would trigger budget increases for education. That would create a quandary for politicians who tend to worry more about cost increases that occur on their watch and less about those that occur after they leave office.

Where Is the Outrage?

The dropout problem has become a widely publicized national issue, but unfortunately it has generated little outrage among the public or parents. We get more media attention and national concern for a few climbers who get stranded on a mountain than for the loss of more than a million kids every year.

A number of organizations have focused on the problem, and some have crafted programs or models designed to reduce the number of dropouts. Politicians have passed legislation designed to address the dropout problem. In 2009, for example, U.S. Representative George Miller (D-California), chair of the House Education and Labor Committee, introduced a bill to improve the nation's lowest-performing middle and high schools. The bill, the Graduation for All Act, would commit $2 billion to transform the 2,000 or so "dropout factories" that fail to graduate more than 40 percent of their seniors (Gewertz, 2009). Like other efforts to solve the dropout problem, this bill would provide guidance to districts on how to turn around failing schools, and it would provide support for at-risk students. The bill would help districts develop data systems to identify potential dropouts based on indicators such as skipping or failing core courses.

In what seems like a contradiction in the bill, Congressman Miller proposes to "combine rigorous coursework with academic and social support services to encourage students and keep them engaged in school" (Educational Publishing, 2009). That sounds like more of the same standards-based accountability exemplified by No Child Left Behind, which the congressman championed in the House at the beginning of the decade.

We can only wish Mr. Miller success. But like most other dropout-prevention programs (on which the nation has spent hundreds of millions of dollars), this new bill largely accepts the conventional school model and tries to fix it.

That is the main reason that none of the many previous fixes have worked; they do not address the profound flaws in the way the conventional school is organized and operated. After-school programs, mentors, internships, and school-to-work programs may have positive effects on some young people, but they are basically attempts to bail out a badly leaking boat.

A 2006 Civic Enterprises study of the problem—*The Silent Epidemic*—noted that the relatively few federal evaluations of "promising practices, programs, and policies" in more than 100 dropout-prevention programs found "that most programs did not reduce dropout rates by statistically significant amounts" (Bridgeland, DiIulio, & Burke Morison, 2006, p. 19).

Dropping Out Starts Early

It should be clear by now that we will not solve the dropout problem with prevention programs. We must understand and focus on why students choose to leave school. Dropping out is not an impulsive decision. The process begins long before high school, often by the 4th or 5th grade. More often than not it is rooted in the failure of students to learn to read—not just to decode the English language, but to read and understand what they read.

Decoding may get children through the Dick and Jane books that have few abstract words (e.g., Dick throws the ball). But with books that begin to deal with ideas and concepts, the ability simply to decode is insufficient. A number of studies have shown that children can read fluently aloud from a text yet fail to explain the meaning of what they read. NAEP scores indicate that only about a quarter of 4th graders can read proficiently, and there has been no significant improvement in grades 8 and 12.

Youngsters who do not read for comprehension will not do well in history or geography or science, or even math. They may be held back a year or barely pass to the next grade. Because they fail early and often, they come to accept failure as inevitable.

The majority of students who plan to drop out have made up their minds by the 8th grade and mark time until they reach the legal age, which is generally 16. Some studies indicate that about a third of dropouts leave in the 9th grade (*Education Week*, 2007).

Students drop out for a variety of reasons. Boredom is a leading cause. Some years ago, a survey of students asked them what word they would use to best describe school; "boring" won hands down. Just because students are consistently bored doesn't mean they can't learn, but rather that they aren't motivated to do so. They have the ability to succeed in school. They explain their decision to leave by saying they find school to be a "waste of time" and complain that school doesn't challenge them.

In the Civic Enterprises study mentioned earlier, two-thirds of the students said they would have worked harder if more had been demanded of them, but they also said they were not motivated or inspired to work harder. And nearly half of student dropouts responding said they were leaving school because classes were not interesting and they could not "connect" to the school (Bridgeland, Dilulio, & Burke Morison, 2006, pp. 4–5).

Raise the Bar, Increase the Dropouts

These reasons, advocates of standards-based accountability argue, show the need for tougher standards and more demanding courses. But it is at least equally probable that the students are saying that the content of the courses does not interest them or the courses are poorly taught. It's not that they want tougher courses but rather more interesting and relevant courses that challenge them to think.

In the Civic Enterprises survey, 35 percent of the students responding said they dropped out because they couldn't keep up with their schoolwork and therefore failed repeatedly; and about 45 percent blamed poor preparation in earlier schooling. Many students gave personal reasons, such as the need to earn money or care for a parent, or because they became parents themselves (Bridgeland, Dilulio, & Burke Morison, 2006, pp. 4–7).

A report released by the California Dropout Research Project (CDRP) linked dropping out of school with health problems that often cause students to miss many days of school (Breslau, 2010).

The American Medical Association reports that about 25 percent of the nation's children have chronic health problems (Steenhuysen, 2010).

As noted earlier, millions of dollars have been spent on dropout-prevention plans without much success because they do not fundamentally address the school problems that lead to more dropouts. Once upon a time, the rearing of children was a responsibility shared jointly by the family, the church, and the school. Now, for many kids, none of those institutions is doing a great job. To help students cope with personal problems and the demands of their out-of-school lives, a handful of outlier schools have developed various support services for students, abandoned inflexible schedules, and kept schools open well into the evening.

But the vast majority of schools are preoccupied with standards, tests, core curricula, and rigorous courses. Their main concern is academics, and their paramount objective is for students to get good grades and passing test scores and have a good shot at getting into college. That is as it should be, many would say. But school is about more than academics or we would not have interscholastic sports or other extracurricular activities or vocational education. Policymakers and education leaders need to question whether the emphasis on academic rigor actually prompts many students to leave school.

A peer-reviewed study published early in 2008 in *Education Policy Analysis Archives* (McSpadden McNeil, Coppola, Radigan, & Vasquez Heilig, 2008) notes that Texas was the model for the high-stakes test accountability of No Child Left Behind and reports that 135,000 teenagers are lost from Texas high schools every year. More than 60 percent of them are African American and Latino. Based on extensive ethnographic analysis, it is clear that the state's high-stakes tests directly increase the severity of the dropout problem. Although NCLB and states claim that the disaggregation of student scores by race leads to more equity, the report insists that instead it "puts our most vulnerable youth—the poor, the English language learners, and African American and Latino children—at risk of being pushed out of their schools so the school ratings can show 'measurable improvement'" (McSpadden McNeil et al., 2008, "Abstract," para. 1).

As I was reviewing the final editing of this chapter on Sunday, August 15, 2010, the *Providence Journal* carried a front-page story warning that higher standards and tough new tests may keep thousands of Rhode Island high school seniors from graduating in June 2012. This year's 11,000 juniors, who will take new high-stakes exams in October 2010, "will be the first to pay the price of the more rigorous diploma system."

If the new diploma system had been in full effect the last two years, nearly half of the state's juniors would have been at risk of not graduating because of poor performance on the math portion of the state tests. Forty-five percent of juniors scored in the lowest possible category, "substantially below proficient."

The "Just Say Stay" Policy

Trying to talk students into staying in school with the "just say stay" approach rarely works. Legislation that forces potential dropouts to stay in school for an extra year or two is cruel and unusual punishment and is likely to be counterproductive. If students leave school because they feel they are not learning, are constantly failing, or because they have personal problems outside of school, how can we possibly think it makes sense to demand they stay for another year or two? Policymakers and education leaders need to question whether higher standards, more rigorous courses, and tougher high-stakes tests are the right strategies for reducing dropout rates.

To repeat: The get-tough approach of NCLB has not worked. It hasn't closed the achievement rate or increased the graduation rate. In fact, the dropout rate has held steady or increased slightly since 1990.

| CHAPTER 8 |

Time for What?

ASSUMPTION: *Making the school day and school year longer will increase student learning.*

The assumption about lengthening the amount of time spent in school followed logically from *A Nation at Risk* and led to calls across the country that continue to the present for a longer school year and school day. But more time in school will not improve achievement if the time is not spent productively. To assume that students will learn more in schools if only they spend more time there is nonsense.

Some districts added time to the school schedule in the mid-1980s without boosting student performance. Not long ago, the *Miami Herald* provided a more timely example, reporting on a district study of a three-year, $100 million plan designed to improve student achievement at 39 Miami-area schools through the implementation of a longer school day, a longer school year, and an intensive reading program (McGrory, 2009). The district conceded that the plan had very little effect on student test scores. Instead, students as well as teachers were worn out by the extra time and work, the report found, and students in the targeted schools actually scored worse on state tests in writing, math, and science than peers in schools without the program. To add more time to schooling without implementing the significant changes necessary to make that time productive is a waste of both time and money.

In recent years, just lengthening the school day or year has begun giving way to the concept of linking the amount of time spent to the way it is used. Generally known as "expanded learning time," this approach uses time to advance school improvement measures. A National Center for Time and Learning has been established to promote the idea.

Senator Edward Kennedy introduced a bill to spend $50 million in federal funds on expanded learning time programs. A recent report found that a number of states are already experimenting with expanded school schedules. Districts in Portland, Oregon; Seattle, Washington; Miami–Dade County, Florida; West Fresno, California; and Pittsburgh, Pennsylvania, have expanded school schedules (Collaborative for Building After-School Systems, 2008). Proposals are being considered in Connecticut, Delaware, Illinois, Indiana, Minnesota, Missouri, Nebraska, Pennsylvania, Utah, and Washington (After-School Corporation, 2008).

Massachusetts is implementing a pilot project run by a nonprofit organization called Massachusetts 2020, which requires participating schools to redesign their academic programs to show that they will use the time more effectively to improve student achievement (Massachusetts 2020, 2010). The program expands school schedules by 25 percent. According to the program's guidelines, participating schools and districts have the flexibility to create their own redesign approach, including goals, staffing plans, labor agreements, compensation, and schedules. This flexibility is intended to spur innovation. The redesign is mandated to be tied to student needs, student goals, and a clear schoolwide academic focus. Additional time must be aimed at improving academic outcomes and broadening opportunities in three key areas: (1) core academics; (2) enrichment opportunities; and (3) teacher planning and professional development.

State officials report that the Expanded Learning Time (ELT) initiative is having a positive and promising effect on parents, teachers, and student performance; and nearly three-quarters of parents and teachers surveyed believe it's having a positive effect on the participating students. ELT officials say the redesign of the school day has translated into improvement trends across all tested subjects. In 2009, all participating schools saw achievement gains in English language arts (ELA), math, and science compared with the state averages. Specifically, these schools gained in proficiency at double the rate of the state in ELA and math and gained at nearly five times the rate of the state in science across all grades.

The results of the Massachusetts pilot program have been impressive. But they would be even more impressive if the measure of success went beyond test scores. Correlation between real student learning and better scores on standardized tests is yet to be proven.

Using Time More Effectively

As noted, a case can be made for a longer school year or school day if the added time is used more effectively. Reformers have long been pointing to other countries where students spend more time in school than American students. On average, a student in the United States attends school 6.5 hours a day for 180 days, far less than is customary in many European and Asian countries. Moreover, much of the day in U.S. schools is not spent on learning but on changing classes, taking roll, and other noninstructional activities (Time, Learning, and Afterschool Task Force, 2007).

Even if expanding the school schedule is shown to improve student learning, however, the shift will be controversial. The traditional school day of five or six periods of about 50 minutes each in various academic subjects is almost set in stone. Attempts at block scheduling, for instance, have been controversial and generally have not produced the desired results. In many instances unions have negotiated restrictions on lengthening the school day, and they are not likely to agree without additional compensation.

These reasons alone make the cost involved in adding more hours to the school schedule significant, depending on the amount of time added and what the funds are used for. The ELT initiative in Massachusetts adds 300 hours to the schedule and increases the per-pupil expenditure by $1,300 (Massachusetts 2020, 2010). If all states followed suit, the average national per-pupil costs presumably would go up by 25 percent, or about $2,500—from about $10,000 to about $12,500, for an additional cost nationally of about $135 billion.

I'm not opposed to a longer school day or year, but I don't think a minute or a day should be added to the schedule without first carefully considering how every minute and day in school is spent. Neither the conventional school schedule nor what goes on in schools has changed much over the past century. We should begin by assessing what schools do in the context of what challenges the new century poses.

One of the pressures for lengthening the school year and school day is related to the demands of the standards movement to accommodate the existing standards. Midcontinent Research for Education and Learning found in a study that there is not enough time in the present calendar to do the job. The report concludes: "If American educators were to adequately cover all of the knowledge identified in the current set of standards for the core subject areas, it might take as much as 22 years of schooling (literally!) within the current structure" (Marzano & Kendall, 1998, p. 1).

Time for Personal Growth

Policymakers and educators tend to think that school is all about academics. We might also consider formal schooling in the context of personal growth and development and the way that adolescents become productive and responsible adults. The prominent sociologist James Coleman chaired a commission on transition to adulthood that issued its report in 1974, in which it states the following:

> As the labor of children has become unnecessary to society, school has been extended for them. With every decade, the length of schooling has increased, until a thoughtful person must ask whether society can conceive of no other way for youth to come into adulthood. If schooling were a complete environment, the answer would probably be that no amount of school is too much, and increased schooling for the young is the best way for the young to spend their increased leisure and society its increased wealth.

Who among us thinks today's public school is "a complete environment"?

Fortunately, some states and organizations are considering such programs to use time in other than the traditional ways. *Learning Around the Clock: Benefits of Expanded Learning Opportunities for*

Older Youth, a report by the American Youth Policy Forum (Bowles & Brand, 2009), suggests that expanded learning opportunities encompass a range of programs and activities available to young people that occur beyond regular school hours and include after-school activities, internships with employers, independent study in alternative settings, and dual-enrollment programs that permit students to finish high school in three years, attend college courses while they are in high school, and earn a high school diploma and associate arts degree at the same time. The report describes key program elements that lead to successful outcomes, such as experiential learning, high-quality staff with ongoing professional development, student-centered programming, and supportive adult and peer-to-peer relations.

Time is critically important in education, and efforts like those just mentioned deviate from the orthodoxy and will be hard won. They point in a new and promising direction. A rational school improvement strategy would decide how time should be spent before addressing how much of it is needed.

| CHAPTER 9 |

Never Enough Money

ASSUMPTION: *If we invest more money in public schools, we will be able to provide every student with an excellent education.*

Public education, it seems, is always about money. Ask the people in charge why they can't increase student learning, close the achievement gap between rich and poor, and reduce the dropout rate, and the answer is always the same: We don't have enough money.

This funding shortfall seems to exist even though the United States spends more on public schools than any other nation in the world. In 2008–09, the latest figure available, we spent about $611 billion on public K–12 education—over 4 percent of the gross national product (NCES, 2009a). The National Center for Education Statistics reports that the national average per-pupil expenditure is about $10,000. The range goes from close to $16,000 per pupil in New York ($21,000 in Long Island) to just under $6,000 in Utah.

In recent years, I have heard more than one prominent educator speculate from the podium about whether our current system is financially sustainable. Is there a limit to the proportion of the nation's wealth that can or should be spent on education? Is there some point at which taxpayers will simply cry "enough!"? Indeed, how do those running the system define enough? Nobody seems to know.

The case for more money would be easier to make if there were persuasive evidence that additional funding would lead to increased student learning. But there isn't. Studies find that how we spend available education resources is at least as important as *how much* we spend on education. The system seems to concentrate only on how much. When education dollars are hard to come by, schools do not undertake a systematic analysis of costs and benefits. Instead, they tend to cut extracurricular activities or field trips or the arts— expenditures that I believe yield a decent return for the dollar.

The most egregious example I've seen in a long time of cutting funding for worthy projects to sustain a mediocre system is occurring in Providence, Rhode Island, as I write this. About five years ago, Hope High School was a low-performing school with low attendance and high dropout rates, low morale, and serious discipline problems. It was so bad that the state schools chief appointed a master to turn the school around. Nick Donohue, now head of the Nellie Mae Education Foundation, worked with the staff and students to accomplish that daunting task. The school divided itself into three separate academies and adopted a block schedule, student advisories, and common planning time for teachers.

I was skeptical that the turnaround would work, but the changes took root and began to pay off. Hope improved steadily and significantly. It appeared to be on its way to becoming what reformers say an urban high school should be.

But no good deed goes unpunished. In response to the state's financial woes and budget cuts, the Providence superintendent announced that the cost of maintaining the new Hope was too high; more than 20 additional teachers were needed, at a cost of $2.5 million. Therefore, the superintendent told the Board of Regents, the reforms would be rolled back. Common planning time for teachers and student advisories would be sharply reduced. Block scheduling would end.

A *Providence Journal* report (Borg, 2010) of students appealing to the Board of Regents to continue the reforms said, "The [new] arts program at Hope High School, with its deep ties to the Rhode Island School of Design, was nothing short of a revelation for many students, who found their voices in theater or the fine arts or the spoken word."

One tearful student said, "Poetry has changed my life. I'm not a good writer, but poetry let me find my identity. I can't tell you how much Hope means to me."

What is this school reform movement all about? Why would policymakers and educators demand high standards and better schools, then cut funding for a low-performing school when it begins to improve? That would be a good example of a "race to the bottom" policy.

Spend on What Works

If we continue to spend money on a school model that doesn't work instead of one that does, we will continue to need ever more education funding and will continue to get poor results.

The Organization for Economic Cooperation and Development concluded in 2008 that learning outcomes in member countries could be increased by more than 20 percent with current funding. "Learning outcomes" is probably a euphemism for test scores, but, even so, a 20 percent jump in scores would make educators think they'd died and gone to heaven.

The conclusion that schools could accomplish more with what they spend is buttressed by the assertion from school-finance experts that those spending the money do not know with any exactitude where the dollars go, what they buy, or whether or how they make a difference in learning. Without answers to those questions, educators and policymakers cannot make changes in traditional schools that may enable them to improve student learning at less cost.

Jacob E. Adams, director of the School Finance Redesign Project at the University of Washington, told *Education Week* that "public school finance systems today uniformly fail to support the nation's education goals regarding greater student performance." He added: "Finance systems determine the levels of support based on political bargaining rather than student needs, and local finance systems are so convoluted that district leaders really don't know where the money is going at the nuts-and-bolts level, where it counts" (Olson, 2005, para. 4).

Over the past 40 years, all but six states have been challenged in court over their school-funding programs—usually on the basis of inequity (Rebell & Baker, 2009). The U.S. Supreme Court has weighed in on some key cases. Judicial decisions have been mixed, and the demand for equity remains largely unmet. Perhaps as a result, the emphasis recently shifted from equity to adequacy. Plaintiffs argue that if students are required to meet high academic standards to be promoted or to graduate, then public schools are obligated to provide them with an education that is adequate for them to accomplish that.

A number of states have hired consultants to study the issue and help them define adequacy. That means calculating specifically how much it costs to provide the "thorough and efficient" education that most state constitutions require. After 35 years of legal battles, the New Jersey Supreme Court approved a new funding formula in May 2009 that seems to meet that requirement. The court determined that students are constitutionally entitled to an educational opportunity that is needed in the contemporary setting to "equip a child for his role as a citizen and as a competitor in the labor market" (Rebell & Baker, 2009, para. 12).

That judicial mandate is only slightly more specific than "thorough and efficient." Its stated goal was to "ensure that all children in all communities have the opportunity to succeed" (New Jersey Department of Education, 2007, p. 4). What is specifically needed to provide the opportunity for every student to succeed, including those with additional needs? How much would it cost per student? To answer such questions, New Jersey, with the expert advice of panels of professionals, spent five years defining the specifics of a funding formula that would equitably serve all children.

There is no doubt that court-ordered funding formulas have exposed inequities in many school districts and have increased education costs. They probably have reduced inequities and improved schools, but by how much is not clear. Poorer districts in some states have reported higher test scores, but as we noted in Chapter 3, the way states score their tests does not always reflect reality.

Considering how long we've been operating public schools and how much we spend on them, one might understandably be stunned that experts, educators, and policymakers have spent the past couple of decades struggling to define what constitutes an adequate education or even agree on the best way to find out.

Whether the emphasis on adequacy produces the desired results remains to be seen. The proof is in the outcomes. Insufficient funding and unwise allocation of funds prevent schools from fulfilling even their fundamental mission. Flawed formulas and those not implemented well result in inequity.

The conundrum is that if we can't define an adequate education and agree on it, then how can we determine what it costs or how to allocate funds to achieve it? Even more disconcerting is the fact that we really don't know with any precision where the education dollars go or even whether they are being spent effectively to increase student learning. How can the public take seriously the ubiquitous complaint that "we don't have enough money"? And even if that were true, where is the money to come from?

Is the System Financially Sustainable?

A few years ago the *Providence Journal* published an op-ed I wrote presenting many of the points made above. Shortly afterward, the mayor of Providence asked me to meet with him. He said he agreed with my analysis, adding that "to provide the funds the schools want, I would need at least an additional $25 million a year from the state." Good luck with that, I thought. Acknowledging the political impossibility of such an increase, he asked: Could the system be reformed to work without major increases in funding? I heard an echo from the trenches of what scholars had been saying at education conferences: Is the system as it now exists financially sustainable in the long term?

My guess is that it isn't. And though I am not an economist and know little about school budgeting, I do know that the present model is labor intensive, with more than 60 cents of each dollar going to pay teaching staff and most of the rest for support services—items that will certainly increase with inflation. The central question should not be about the amount of money required but what it buys. If productivity does not increase along with costs, taxpayers may look for more efficient ways to educate their children.

The new-schools strategy I advocate in this book will not be cheap. Indeed, it might even be more costly than the existing school system. But I am convinced it would be better and would produce the outcomes that society and children desire. Isn't it better to pay more for high quality, if necessary, than to pay almost as much for mediocrity? If all of our children were truly well educated, the financial return to the society would far exceed the cost of education.

| CHAPTER 10 |

A New Strategy of New Schools

ASSUMPTION: *It is unwise and unnecessary to bet everything on the standards-based accountability strategy; we should simultaneously embark on a second strategy of creating innovative, small schools.*

The definition of insanity, Albert Einstein is reputed to have said, is "doing the same thing over and over again and expecting different results." That pretty well describes the current 30-year effort to reform schools.

Nearly all of the ideas, programs, and policies to improve schools have been based on faulty assumptions about learning, kids, teachers, curriculum, assessment, and every other aspect of education. It follows naturally that if the assumptions underlying our education system are wrong, then our efforts to change or improve that system will be ineffective or, even worse, counterproductive.

The only useful basis on which to evaluate a strategy or a course of action is whether it is achieving its goals. Is it working?

By that measure, standards-based reform as a national school improvement strategy (epitomized by No Child Left Behind) is unsuccessful. Despite nudging the system upward slightly here and there, the strategy has not significantly improved schools. After more than two decades of intense effort,

- It has not increased overall student achievement or student learning or closed the gap for poor and minority students.
- It has not prepared most students who earn a diploma for either college or the workplace.

- It has not reduced the dropout rate.
- It has not responded effectively to the diversity of today's student body.
- It has not improved the quality of teachers or principals.
- It has not improved the programs that prepare teachers and principals.
- It has not made the use of either time or money in education more efficient.
- It has not exploited the new technology.

What has standards-based accountability accomplished? Little more than grade-level academic standards in the states and greatly increased testing, including high-stakes standardized tests that have put considerable pressure on schools and students without achieving positive outcomes. Despite this, the proponents of standards-based accountability propose to intensify their efforts by establishing common national standards, a national curriculum, and international benchmarks. The theory of operations seems to be "If it doesn't work, do more of it and do it harder."

I've come to believe that it is futile to try to reverse that strategy. Too many have too much ego and effort invested in it to persuade them at this point to abandon it or substantially change it. In an open letter to the governors and prominent business leaders on the occasion of the 1999 "education summit," I argued that we desperately need a course correction. I spelled out the reasons as persuasively as I knew how, and the letter was included in the book of readings prepared for the participants. As far as I know, it sank like a stone. But during the following year, Secretary of Education Dick Riley in a national speech called for a "course correction" in the standards movement. He made about as much progress as I had.

The Need for a Parallel Strategy

Standards-based accountability is here to stay—at least for a long time.

So the only other rational response I can think of is to adopt a parallel strategy and pursue it simultaneously—what my friend Ted Kolderie (2010) calls "a split-screen" approach to improving education. Why should we bet everything on a single strategy, especially if it isn't working? Why not have at least one alternative strategy? Why not have parallel strategies that seek to achieve the same objectives? Why can't we walk and chew gum at the same time?

We have already begun in piecemeal fashion to develop a second strategy of creating new, innovative schools. These schools not only offer more choices to students, but also they have the potential to promote change and improvement in the existing system by serving informally as a research and development arm for traditional schools.

Although not conceived as a strategy, the movement to create new schools alongside traditional schools began to take shape at the end of the 1980s with two major innovations. One was a policy innovation; the other involved new technologies.

In 1991, Minnesota enacted the nation's first chartering law, which, for the first time in history, delegated to nongovernmental agencies the authority to establish publicly funded schools (Schroeder, 2004). Shortly afterward, City School in St. Paul became the nation's first charter school.

A year earlier, in 1990, the World Wide Web was born as a network for the exchange of ideas and information. It was intended also to capitalize on an expanding Internet and create an online library of knowledge. But the Internet/Web at first was like a library with all the books dumped haphazardly in the middle of the reading room. The 1990s produced several limited search engines, and in 1997, Google created a highly successful one that brought order and efficiency to the situation and a world of information to the user.

These developments were largely unnoticed by the public at the time, and few foresaw the effect they would have on education. Not many educators were using computers, let alone connecting them to the Internet. *Education Week* didn't hire a technology reporter until 1993, and he couldn't explain the Internet in a way that I could understand. We were a bit quicker in covering the charter movement, and our first story on charter schools in 1991 reported the progress of the St. Paul City School in obtaining the first charter.

Some 20 years later, there is growing realization that these innovations have enormous potential to advance learning and to change the way students are educated. Nonetheless, their promise remains largely unfulfilled.

Forty states and the District of Columbia had adopted chartering laws by the end of 2009; some 5,000 chartered schools enrolled more than 1.5 million students, according to the Center for Education Reform in Washington, D.C. (2009a). Given the size of the education establishment, that is the equivalent of a toe in the door.

Promising Innovations: Technology and Chartering

The number of computers in schools has increased steadily, and connectivity to the Internet has become commonplace. But few could argue persuasively that technology has been integrated into the school culture in ways that really exploit its potential.

Chartering and the Web, though still fledgling efforts, have laid the foundations for a second strategy of creating new educational opportunities that put students and learning first. But even if the strategy of starting new and different schools gains momentum rapidly, the schools will enroll only a small fraction of the total student body for many years to come. Large, complicated systems change only incrementally, if at all. Innovations and best practices do not spread easily or quickly, especially in public education.

That reality means the existing schools will remain the only option for the vast majority of American students, and it is imperative, therefore, that we continue and intensify our efforts to improve the schools we have. A second strategy can help if it encourages innovation and helps build an infrastructure to facilitate the spread of ideas and practices.

Some people oppose a new-schools strategy, arguing that scarce resources would be devoted to new schools when there is growing pressure to cut education budgets. States and school districts can mitigate the effect if they have the will and courage to close the lowest-performing schools and replace them with new educational opportunities to serve the students who attended those schools.

Closing schools is a politically perilous step. Communities usually rise in protest, even when the school designated for closure is terrible. Michelle Rhee, the feisty and controversial former superintendent of public schools in the District of Columbia, told of visiting a school where only 10 percent of students were reading at grade level. As she left, she stopped to talk with a group of men on a corner across from the school—most of whom probably had attended the school. "What do you think of this school?" she asked. The response was unanimously favorable: good school, good principal and teachers.

The story illustrates the saying that "we must not love our schools more than we love our children." The school in question is a "lousy school," but to the community, it is *their* school. They must be helped to see the harm it is doing to their children, and they need to know that a better option exists. Toxic schools should either be transformed or closed. If education leaders fail to make that choice, then policymakers should make it for them.

In his book *The Innovator's Dilemma*, Clayton Christensen (2003) documents the demise of Fortune 500 companies that went out of business because they failed to adapt and change in response to a disrupting innovation that spawned competition. As an example, he cites Digital Equipment Corporation (DEC), which was immensely profitable as the main producer of expensive, large, mainframe computers. When Apple introduced its first computer, it was little more than a toy. DEC could have produced desktop computers, but officials ignored the new Apple and continued on their course. Eventually, personal computers could do everything mainframes could do at far less cost, and Digital went out of business.

In a subsequent book, *Disrupting Class* (Christensen, Horn, & Johnson, 2008), Christensen and his coauthors offer DEC (and other examples) as an object lesson for educators. In ignoring or opposing innovations, the public education system puts itself in peril of going out of business.

In the earlier chapters of this book, we challenged the major assumptions on which education in the United States is based. The new, innovative schools—both charters and district schools—that result from a second strategy must be based on a different set of assumptions. And the overriding assumption is that the challenge is not to reform the school but to redesign it.

The existing school model was not designed to meet the needs and challenges of the new century. We are blaming it for not doing what it was never intended to do. And we are trying to solve our educational problems by making incremental improvements in an obsolete model, even though it must now be obvious that tinkering will not make that model work much better.

Assumptions for a New Strategy

In the following pages I offer alternative assumptions on which a new-schools strategy should be based. These assumptions may not have been widely tested, but both research and anecdotal evidence suggest that they improve student learning. They should be studied, debated, and piloted. Although some aspects of these assumptions have not been implemented widely enough to guarantee that they will work for a majority of students, they offer more promise than the flawed assumptions that underlie the present system.

I have always found it odd that we tend to reject new or different approaches in education on the grounds that we do not have proof that they will work and, therefore, to apply them would be to use our children as guinea pigs. What parents would refuse an experimental treatment if their child was suffering an incurable disease?

Why should new ideas bear the burden of proof when the existing system is allowed to continue essentially unchanged even though it is largely failing? If we don't try new ideas and alternative approaches, how will we ever know if they work?

It is an irrefutable fact that the existing schools are failing to educate a substantial proportion of American students. I find it hard to imagine that a new strategy would be any riskier or less effective than the system we now have. Former American Federation of Teachers leader Al Shanker used to say that if a delegation of Martians visited earth to see how we educate our children, they would think we were crazy.

PART 2

A SECOND, PARALLEL STRATEGY

| CHAPTER 11 |

One Student at a Time

ASSUMPTION: *To help motivate children and maximize their abilities, we must educate them one at a time and tailor their education to their interests and needs.*

The engine of a new-schools strategy is personalized education. It shapes virtually every aspect of schooling. For example, schools must be relatively small because students and teachers must know each other well if education is to be personalized. Such a model has no traditional core curriculum with typical academic courses and rigid schedules because standardization is the antithesis of personalization. Students play a significant role in designing their own curriculum, which usually emphasizes real-world learning. Traditional instruction and textbooks are minimized, and teachers become advisors who guide students in educating themselves, tutor them, and help them manage their time and energy. Because bubble-in standardized tests to evaluate students are incompatible with personalized education, student learning is assessed on the basis of actual work as demonstrated in portfolios, exhibitions, special projects, and experiments, recitals, and performances—real accomplishments rather than abstract test scores.

That's it in a nutshell. Personalization embodies the assumptions (premises) on which a new-schools strategy should be based. Today's students come from different socioeconomic situations and cultural backgrounds, learn in different ways and at different speeds, and have different talents, problems, and aspirations. To accommodate this enormous student diversity, the strategy should encourage the creation of new schools that are different from conventional schools and from each other, and they should offer a variety of educational opportunities.

Personalized education is taking root in other countries. Great Britain's Department for Children, Schools, and Families, for example, has adopted *The Children's Plan*, which is based on the premise of personalized education. Its director writes:

> In the best schools in the country, excellent classroom practice has already established a pedagogy and culture of personalized teaching and learning. Our new approach in schools—which looks at progression across stages—means we will focus on every pupil, in every year group, not just those at the end of key stages and in the middle of the ability range. (Department for Children, Schools, and Families, 2007, p. 63)

The concept has even begun to appear in the United States in recent years. Rhode Island is the first state to commit to personalization by mandating that every child have an individualized learning plan beginning in the 6th grade (McWalters, 2005). Other states and districts are moving toward some version of personalization.

The movement got a boost when *Breaking Ranks*, one of the best reports to be published during the current school improvement effort, recommended personalization. The 1996 report by the National Association of Secondary School Principals urged that large high schools break into units of no more than 600 students, with each teacher responsible for no more than 90 students. The report called for schools to provide individual learning plans and "personal adult advocates" for every student. Teachers should adapt their instruction to accommodate individual learning styles, the report said.

Beginning in 2000, the Bill and Melinda Gates Foundation began to fund small, innovative schools across the country. Proof of concept for personalized education was soon well established, and the philosophy began to spread. Many of the Gates-supported small schools have replicated themselves across the country. Big Picture Learning, which designed and established The Met in Providence, has a network of more than 70 Big Picture schools in the United States and abroad based on its model. Similarly, EdVisions, creator of Minnesota New Country School, has since established nearly 50 schools in its image. EdVisions schools are unique in that they are owned and operated by teachers, much as the old agricultural co-op was, or as group practices in law and medicine are today.

Ending the "Monolithic Batch" System

Obviously, we still have a very long way to go. Clayton Christensen warns in *Disrupting Class*, "If we acknowledge that all children learn differently, then the way schooling is currently arranged—in a monolithic batch mode system where all students are taught the same things on the same day in the same way—won't ever allow us to educate children in customized ways" (Christensen, Horn, & Johnson, 2008, p. 225). And I would add, "as they should."

Schools are required by law to provide all special-needs students with individual learning plans because they are "different." Well, *every child* is different and every child deserves an individual learning plan. Education should adopt the medical model: treat all patients as individuals; diagnose their specific health problem using selected tests to pinpoint conditions; prescribe a specific treatment; and use results to assess progress and success.

Some will insist that this is impractical. How can we educate millions of students in small schools and provide them with a personalized education? New York City, the nation's largest school district, adopted a policy in 2002 to close big conventional high schools and replace them with 200 small schools by 2010. That has been accomplished, and according to a recent report (Quint, Smith, Unterman, & Moedano, 2010), the new schools were serving almost as many students as the closed big schools had served. If you can do it in New York, as the lyrics go, you can do it anywhere.

Personalization is only impractical in conventional schools where all students are force-marched through a rigid, comprehensive curriculum every day—and that is exactly the point. We have built an elaborate and expensive education system on the assumption that it is more important to teach children what we think they should know than it is to help them learn what they want to learn and build on that. Such an approach is a formula for failure, and all the data document that failure. Personalized education is practiced successfully in innovative small schools that are devoted to teaching students and not just curricula.

Although every child should have an individual learning plan, the first priority of a new-schools strategy must be the two-thirds or more of the students who are being poorly served by the existing system. A major mission of any new strategy is to make equity in education a reality, a promise that is unfulfilled even though the U.S. Supreme Court made school desegregation illegal more than half a century ago. The pioneering schools in this new strategy—both chartered and district schools—are already demonstrating this commitment by reaching out to poor, minority, and immigrant students who are generally the most at risk of academic failure.

Most of these students have the ability to learn, but too often they lack the opportunity and the motivation. As noted in Chapter 7, a great many students dropped out of school because they were bored or alienated by the conventional school and had little if any motivation to attend or do the work required of them. For a significant number, personal or family problems made it difficult if not impossible to conform to the conventional demands of the typical school.

Much of the emphasis of the current reform movement is on better teaching, better instruction. But we know that no matter what we teach, students will not learn what they don't want to learn. Some students who aspire to attend college may have no interest in learning what they are being taught in some courses, but they do their best to memorize what they need to know to pass their courses. Given the high percentage of college freshmen who need to take remedial courses, it is likely that many forget a lot of what they learned in high school before the ink on their diplomas is dry. (Or, more likely, they never learned it in the first place.)

I once listened to a 7th grade student in rural North Carolina read from a geography textbook. He read easily and fluently. But when asked by the teacher to elaborate on what he'd just read, he had not a clue. He had learned to decode, but he did not have enough interest in geography to care about what he was reading.

Later I saw him on a bench eating his lunch and reading a magazine about guns. I sat down and we began to talk. Before long, he was holding forth with great enthusiasm about what he'd just read. He was knowledgeable and articulate. Although I wished he'd found geography more interesting than guns, I was convinced that his interest in guns could lead to broader interests in other fields. Weapons have a strong connection to geography if one has the opportunity and encouragement to explore it. A student's interest in weapons can be used to make geography, history, and literature more relevant and interesting.

Personalization Equals Motivation

Evidence and experience suggest that personalization is a key factor in student motivation. Because students learn best when they are interested in the material, schools should focus on their strongest interests and use that as a foundation to build on. A child's interest in collecting rocks can become a lifelong hobby and also be the beginning of a career in science, and learning to play the guitar can spark an enduring interest in music and open the world of the arts and humanities.

Minnesota New Country School in Henderson, Minnesota, is predicated on the belief that students are more motivated and learn best when they are pursuing a personal interest. The heart of the school is project-based education. There is no curriculum, no principal; teachers run the school. Instead of traditional classrooms, each student has a workplace in an office-like setting. Every student has a computer, but books are everywhere. Students work alone or in groups, and advisors tutor individual students, often at their workstations.

More than half of each school day is devoted to interdisciplinary "projects." Students design their project and submit a proposal for faculty approval. The proposal asks key questions and requires details about what the student wants to learn, how he plans to do so, and how the project intersects with state standards. The student has to justify the proposal as a legitimate learning experience and show its value to the community, and how much credit he thinks it is worth. Students keep a daily log of how they spend their time. New Country students work with community experts and are evaluated by them on their performance. Students also evaluate themselves, using a performance rubric to rate their work in three areas: critical thinking skills, leadership and innovation, and the quality of their specific work product.

The array of projects at New Country is broad and rich, and each one is an adventure in learning across disciplines. Perhaps its most famous project—one that became international news—involved a field trip into marshlands where students discovered that half the frogs they collected were deformed. The finding stunned the international science community and sparked global investigations to determine the causes.

For his senior project, one student explored optics, including holography and photography. As part of his undertaking, he created two YouTube videos on how to make holograms. Another student interested in ancient Egypt wanted to know more about how and why Egyptians mummified their leaders. So he read extensively about Egyptian culture and set out to mummify a chicken, learning the chemical and other processes used centuries ago.

Ronald J. Newell, in his excellent book *Passion for Learning* (2003), relates a student's educational experience that exemplifies personalization through project-based learning. For his project, a middle school student wanted to know more about skateboarding. (Although in my view that's better than guns, I'm sure it causes some head shaking and cluck-clucking.) The more he learned, the more he became convinced that his community should have a skateboarding park; so he set out to make it a reality. He met with city officials and wrestled with zoning laws. He researched skateboard parks in other communities, drew up construction designs, and prepared spending projections. And in the process, he learned something about politics, government, construction, mathematics, advocacy, and research. He honed his reasoning skills and his ability to formulate a position and defend it. He mostly taught himself by reading and asking questions, and he produced something real and useful to be assessed on. And I'd wager that he will remember what he learned in that project for the rest of his life.

Although these students' learning experiences are not uncommon in the new schools that personalize education, they may suggest that it is easy to motivate students to learn more and to learn material they don't think they care about. It isn't.

Helping Students Educate Themselves

Helping students to "find their passion" and to pursue it is a complex, often discouraging process. A student's interest in guns or skateboards may not be enough to lure him easily into learning math or science or art. But it takes math to do financial projections and to calculate the dimensions of a skateboard park. If the student needs to learn something to complete a project she is deeply interested in, she will learn it because she needs it and it is immediately useful. That cannot be said about most students' adventures in 9th grade algebra.

There will always be some students who will procrastinate or simply refuse to do the work. But the chances of reaching even those students are improved in a school that gives them a say in what they will study, that promotes close relationships with advisors and peers, that emphasizes real-world experience, and that judges students on their work product.

In the unconventional small schools that I am familiar with— especially Big Picture Learning, EdVisions, High Tech High, Urban Academy—the attendance rate is much higher than in neighboring district schools, and graduation rates exceed those in traditional public high schools. The fact that so few students drop out of these schools is an indication that they are successful even with hard-to-reach students.

Youth is a time for exploration, for satisfying curiosity. Who knows what will light the lamp of learning in each child? Finding out and trying to do just that should be the primary mission of schooling.

Unfortunately, more often than not, school sends a different message to students: What we want to teach is more important than what you want to learn.

As I argued in Chapter 8, a conventional curriculum that divides knowledge into disciplinary blocks and crams it into age-based grades in semester-long courses and 50-minute classes is an insurmountable obstacle to personalizing education. The inherent excitement in acquiring knowledge is often minimized or lost by the rigid organization of curriculum. The natural and real-life connections between the disciplines that spark curiosity and those all-too-rare "aha moments" are absent. If one believes that education should be personalized to the benefit of all children, then one has to believe that the current effort to establish a national core curriculum will push American education in exactly the wrong direction.

| CHAPTER 12 |

Many Pathways to Success

ASSUMPTION: *The more educational opportunities available to young people both in and out of school, the more likely they are to find a pathway to success that is compatible with their unique needs and talents.*

By definition, personalizing education requires creating multiple pathways for students to succeed and reach their goals.

Since the GI Bill following World War II, our society has generally defined success as attending college and earning a bachelor's degree. And for most students the only pathway to that goal is to take a sequence of academic programs beginning with the 1st grade and proceeding through a high school diploma and four years of college courses to a bachelor's degree. It is that view of education that drives the national obsession with "rigorous" standards.

In the past two decades the emphasis on earning a college degree has intensified, and public schools act as if their main mission is to prepare every child for college—which essentially means to meet the academic requirements of college admission standards. Although admission requirements vary from college to college, they basically demand that every applicant pass two years of history, four years of English, three years of mathematics (usually including two years of algebra), two years of laboratory science, and a year of arts studies. In addition, test scores, grades, class rank, and teacher recommendations influence admission decisions. Chances of getting admitted may be greater if applicants have participated in extracurricular activities, especially football, basketball, hockey, and other sports. Summing up the situation, former high school principal Rona Wilensky (2007) argues that "the entire K–12 system is skewed toward meeting the needs of those students headed for selective colleges and universities and the way less successful students are funneled into watered-down versions of a college-preparatory curriculum."

College enrollment has been boosted by a continuing effort to make a college education more accessible. The number of two-year colleges has grown, state institutions' fees are comparably lower than private-college tuition, and federal and state governments provide various kinds of financial aid. About 50 percent of high school graduates in the 1970s enrolled in college compared with more than 60 percent in the past decade (NCES, 2009a). Despite this, however, only 30 percent of 27-year-olds in the United States have a bachelor's degree, largely because about half drop out along the way. Compared with other developed nations, the United States ranks just 13th in high school graduation rates, and 18th in college graduation rates (Data360, 2007). There is something terribly wrong with an educational system from which so many participants drop out or earn a diploma unprepared for the real world.

Bachelor's Degree Not Always Needed

Nearly everyone agrees that profound changes in the U.S. economy—the increased impact of new technology, the decline of traditional manufacturing, and the enormous growth of the service sector—have created a workplace where at least a high school education (and preferably some postsecondary education) is needed for all but the most menial jobs. Not every job, however, requires a bachelor's degree.

Millions of jobs in the future—perhaps half of all openings, according to U.S. Department of Labor (2009) statistics—will not be high-skill jobs but may call for some postsecondary education and training. These jobs include, for example, technicians, mid-level managers, police officers, travel agents, and construction workers such as electricians and plumbers.

Jobs that do not require a bachelor's degree can be fulfilling, well paying, and important to the larger society. As John Gardner once stated, when a society does not value both its philosophers and its plumbers, neither its theories nor its pipes will hold water.

A number of surveys of employers in recent years have documented a growing concern on the part of business officials that a majority of high school graduates are inadequately prepared to succeed in the 21st century workforce. Respondents complained that too many lack the basic skills taught in elementary school (particularly in written and oral communication). But they also insisted that too many high school graduates were deficient in teamwork and collaboration skills and in critical thinking and reasoning. The Conference Board and others in a major report put it this way: "The future U.S. workforce is here—and it is woefully ill-prepared for the demands of today's (and tomorrow's) workplace" (2006, p. 9).

It is not the job of public schools—nor should it be—to train students for specific jobs. Indeed, employers commonly assert that if the schools teach students to think and reason—to read, write, do basic math, and display good habits of conduct—they will teach them what they need to know about the specific job.

Letting Students Set Their Own Course

Presumably, for most people, the skills that employers are looking for can be taught in the first eight grades. From then on, students should be able to choose an educational pathway that they believe is compatible with their interests, aspirations, and learning styles. We ought to be offering a variety of educational opportunities and not "delivering" the same education to every high school student.

In a second strategy to improve education, multiple pathways should be available to all students in a single school if it is large enough or among a portfolio of smaller schools or both. To be most successful, multiple pathways should be created at least in high schools (and even perhaps in middle schools) and should be coordinated and integrated with community-based education programs and children's support systems. This approach to education will help prevent students from dropping out and increase their chances of thriving in the modern workplace.

One can imagine a number of possible pathways for students in high school. Here are some possibilities:

- **Traditional college prep.** Some students thrive in the conventional school that emphasizes academics with its courses, classes, and grades; they do well in this environment—especially those who are highly motivated and expect to attend a selective college. This is the well-trod path to college and higher degrees, to white-collar jobs and professional careers. It is an ideal choice for some students, but not for all.

- **Learning communities.** These tend to be small innovative schools where teachers and students share common values and beliefs and learn together and from each other. Students may work individually and in teams on projects or in internships. Learning communities often extend classroom practices into the surrounding community or bring the community into the school. Community members can enrich the academic curriculum with their real-world experience.

- **Career and technical academies.** These schools tend to be linked closely to the workplace, mainly to give students a firsthand opportunity to explore workplace options and serve in a sequence of internships to acquire work-related experience under the guidance of a mentor. Emphasis is on real-world learning—often out of school.

- **Virtual schools.** The explosion of communications technology and the development of the Internet and the World Wide Web have led to the creation of virtual schools. Students do not gather at a specific site but attend the school through their computers and telephones. They usually formulate a personal curriculum in collaboration with their teacher and parents and often work at home. They "meet" with their teachers and fellow students online. Their work is monitored and assessed by the teacher, perhaps using computer-assisted exams.

- **Independent study.** Schools should recognize the success and value of home schooling and provide students an opportunity to design their own educational plan and pursue it independently under the supervision of a teacher or tutor who would help them manage their educational activities, monitor their progress, and evaluate their work.

Independent study would include reading, writing, and research; students would have more opportunity to travel or serve as an apprentice in an area of particular interest.

Whatever their choice, students would not be locked into a pathway and could move to another if they discovered that a different route would serve them better. Students in all of the pathways would be expected to meet high standards, but the standards should reflect as much as possible the nature of the pathway. A student who chooses an independent-study pathway because he is totally absorbed in writing innovative software should not be required to meet the same content standards as the student who chooses the traditional academic pathway on course to becoming a graduate student and a professional mathematician. Performance standards to demonstrate mastery of skills might well be common to all or at least several pathways. Obviously, the curricula and the pedagogy would vary according to the pathway.

Out-of-School Pathways

Because the vast majority of middle and high school students in the United States are denied the opportunity to choose among different educational pathways, a number of programs are designed to help those young people who are failing in school, who have dropped out, or who are unemployed or underemployed. These include after-school programs, adult education programs, and apprenticeships and workplace internships. A key ingredient for success is the collaboration of industry, education, and community organizations.

The move toward creating multiple pathways has been gaining momentum. A number of states are developing multiple pathways for high school, built on the premise that career and technical education—formerly called "vocational education"—can be academically strong. In California, the Coalition for Multiple Pathways is a statewide alliance of more than 140 education, industry, and community organizations dedicated to improving California's high schools and preparing students for postsecondary education and a career. The New York City Department of Education has established the Office of Multiple Pathways, and Vermont's Department of Education has a High School Completion Model. Some states and districts have opened "newcomers schools" to help older English language learners and newcomer youth learn English and achieve a high school diploma or certificate of completion.

Jeannie Oakes of the Ford Foundation and Marisa Saunders of UCLA wrote in an *Education Week* commentary that what distinguishes schools offering multiple pathways "is that they emphasize and extend student-adult relationships—both within the school and outside of it, with members of the larger community—as a way of weaving exemplary practices into a coherent school reform" (2009, para. 7).

A single educational pathway—a one-size-fits-all education, delivered to all students—is simply not compatible with a diverse student body and a complex and rapidly changing world. It ignores the powerful effects of demography and the popular culture—both of which significantly shape today's students—and it virtually disregards what science and decades of experience have revealed about how the brain works and how children learn.

Many efforts to create multiple pathways might be described as a rescue mission to help students who have the most difficulty with the academic track of traditional schools—kids who have dropped out or are in danger of dropping out. A recent example of an innovative and apparently successful effort was provided when the Innosight Institute published *Wichita Public Schools' Learning Centers: Creating a New Educational Model to Serve Dropouts and At-Risk Students* (Mackey, 2010). According to Innosight executive director Michael Horn (a coauthor of *Disrupting Class*), the program is designed to combat the dropout epidemic in the United States.

The research report describes how Wichita combined virtual learning and traditional classroom instruction to help participants earn a high school diploma. At the four dropout-recovery centers in the district, students choose from a wide variety of computer-based courses and work on their own schedule under the direction of certified teachers. Freed from the conventions of the traditional classroom, teachers can spend most of their time working with individual students. They monitor students' learning and evaluate their progress. "Since the program's founding in 1999," the report notes, "the four dropout-recovery centers have collectively helped

974 students that the traditional schools had failed earn their high school diplomas" (Mackey, 2010, p. 16). The program has also prevented students from leaving high school in the first place by allowing them to retake courses they had failed or dropped. The program was considerably less costly per student than the average in the district; during the 2008–09 school year, the program cost roughly $7,307 per pupil compared with the district average of $11,186. Since the program began, the district's graduation rate has risen by more than 8 percentage points.

The Wichita program seems to be working because it fundamentally alters the traditional high school experience. Structure, schedule, curriculum, and instruction have all been adapted to meet students' needs.

A Fancy Term for "Tracking"?

Some people worry that "multiple pathways" is just a fancy term for tracking. That is a legitimate reason to be careful. For many decades, schools "tracked" students based largely on a combination of race, class, and test scores. Affluent and middle-class white kids largely ended up in the academic track that led to college; children from working-class families and a disproportionate percentage of girls ended up in the business track, which led to jobs like clerk, secretary, accountant, or manager; and poor and minority students were generally in the vocational track, which supposedly prepared them to be skilled laborers like mechanics, welders, and plumbers. Dropouts were largely consigned to labor or menial work.

During most of the 19th and early 20th centuries, the role of schools in sorting and tracking students was widely accepted. In 1908, Charles William Eliot, the renowned president of Harvard University, exhorted elementary school teachers to sort their pupils "by their evident or probable destinies" (Krug, 1961). Children of laborers were expected to become laborers and those of professionals would obviously become professionals.

Fortunately, tracking was largely eliminated in public schools, much to the dismay of some educators who argued that putting all students in the same class was unfair to both the bright and the less bright and made life harder for teachers. That's at least partly true. But some research has shown that both the most and the least able students do better in untracked classrooms that are properly structured and have good teachers.

The multiple pathways now being advocated are not tracking. First, a specific pathway is not mandated; second, they are not based on race or IQ or "probable destinies"; third, every pathway is intended to improve students' proficiency in basic skills and help them learn to reason and solve problems. Unlike tracking, pathways give students a say in their own education and a chance to discover and pursue their passions.

| CHAPTER 13 |

Life to Text

ASSUMPTION: *Students will learn more and remember more of what they learned if they learn in real-world contexts, which also reduces boredom and disciplinary problems, stimulates more parental involvement, inspires self-confidence and responsibility in youth, and motivates them to learn.*

Education in real-world contexts is not a new idea. Aristotle wrote, "For the things we have to learn before we can do them, we learn by doing them." Centuries later John Adams echoed the thought when he said, "There are two types of education: One should teach us how to make a living and the other should teach us how to live." Our current education system is doing neither very well.

Arguably, the best model of education in history was the apprenticeship, where the novice learned from the master. The novice learned by doing, by being corrected and tutored by the master. There was no written test, no grade; the success of the apprentice was based on his work as judged by the master.

Real-world learning, often known as experiential learning, was central in the thinking and writing of philosopher John Dewey and his disciples. In his book *Experiential Learning*, Dewey disciple David Kolb (1984) describes learning as a four-step process: (1) watching, (2) thinking, (3) feeling, and (4) doing. Experiential learning advocates believe that education should engage students in meaningful work seeking answers to their own questions, not just memorizing facts and filling out worksheets.

Joseph P. Allen and Claudia W. Allen, both psychologists, are the authors of *Escaping the Endless Adolescence: How We Can Help Our Teenagers Grow Up Before They Grow Old*, published in 2009. In an article in *Education Week*, they state that academic motivation begins to decline in the 5th or 6th grade and declines through the teens. Although the decline is often based on the well-known problems of adolescence, the authors believe it lies "in a profound mismatch between teenage biology and school structure." They further write:

> Modern brain research increasingly confirms what those who work with teenagers have long known: Adolescents are primed for action, stimulation, and relevance. They seek action as they hit peak physical capacities and energy levels; they seek stimulation as the reward centers in their brains develop; and they seek relevance as they gain the capacity to take on adult-like tasks, both mentally and physically. Yet these normal (and healthy) adolescent traits collide head-on not only with the fundamental structure of secondary schooling, but also with evolving societal trends extending the length of the teenage "waiting period" to truly enter and act on the adult world. (Allen & Allen, 2010, para. 3)

If the primary objective is to help students develop reasoning and problem-solving skills, students should be immersed in a total learning situation. They should be encouraged and taught to formulate a hypothesis, plan how to test that theory, carry out the plan, and be able to understand, assess, and explain the results.

An impressive body of research supports real-world/experiential education, but perhaps the case for real-world learning is best made with examples. As I was writing this chapter, NBC Nightly News carried a story on the only ambulance service in the nation run entirely by high school students (Williams & Menounos, 2009). Student volunteers in Darien, Connecticut, operate the city's 24-hour ambulance service every day of the year. Recruited in their freshman year, some 20 student volunteers participate in a three-month training program and, after 150 hours of training, are certified by the state as emergency medical technicians. Operated by Boy Scout Explorer Post 53, the service responds to more than 1,400 calls a year—some of them involving life-and-death situations. Students work with patients, monitoring their vital signs and stabilizing them as much as possible.

Whatever else the young people may remember about their high school days, I have no doubt that their most indelible memories will be their experience with Post 53. They learn something useful and apply it in ways that contribute to the health of their neighbors and the community. And in the process, they develop skills and attitudes rarely learned in classrooms. As one participant said, "When people look you in the eye and say, 'thank you,' it really makes you realize that what you're doing is worth it" (Adams, 2008).

What Kids Can Do

A decade ago, I became involved with a nonprofit organization called What Kids Can Do. Its founder, Barbara Cervone, formerly with the Annenberg Institute, was troubled that young people are so often portrayed by the media in the worst light. She believes that there are countless examples of youngsters doing important and positive work. And she decided to seek them out and make people aware of them.

The seaside community of Lubec, Maine, provided one of the first and best examples of what she had in mind. Lubec was troubled by the declining health of the fishing industry that had supported families there for generations. All but 2 of the 40 sardine factories in the area had shut down. Students at the local high school discussed the situation in their science class, and a handful of them and their teacher held a town meeting to discuss whether aquaculture might help reverse the problem. Few people showed up.

So the students took matters into their own hands and converted an abandoned water-treatment facility into a state-of-the-art wet laboratory where they farmed mussels and raised salmon and trout in purified water beefed up with a homemade brew of nutrients. In their classrooms, the students, with the help of their teachers, devised an experiment that was yielding important data about the best diet for enhancing the roe of sea urchins—an expensive delicacy in Japan. Their work attracted the attention of national aquaculture companies, researchers at the Massachusetts Institute of Technology, and area biotech entrepreneurs. A third to a half of the Lubec high school students soon were involved in related projects, from monitoring toxic algae to designing a way to protect Lubec's vulnerable marina from the ravages of Atlantic storms and seeking a federal grant to fund construction planning.

Cervone had no trouble finding other examples of students learning in real-world situations. A team of teenagers in Oakland designed a plan to revitalize the block around their local subway stop—and learned economics and design principles in the process. In rural Alabama, students published newspapers for communities that had no source of local news. They conducted research, learned to write and edit, and met deadlines. In an animation program in one California high school, students turn out professional-quality productions for which they conceive the story, write the scripts, and draw and photograph the scenes. These youngsters are learning by doing, and what they are doing has real value to the community and a lasting positive effect on each of them.

Learn by Doing

The Met School in Providence, Rhode Island, exemplifies real-world learning perhaps more than any high school in the nation. As it states on its website, "The Met is grounded in the philosophy of educating 'one student at a time,'" and the conviction that "true learning takes place when each student is an active participant in his or her education." Students are encouraged to pursue their interests—"find your passion" is the mantra.

The Met's commitment to real-world learning is based on the belief that "for students to apply their knowledge in real situations, they need to learn in those situations." Almost everything Met students do is in that context. Students gain real-world experience especially through internships that span at least a semester but could run a year or longer, and through individual projects that they design and carry out.

Each student spends at least two days a week out of school in a Learning Through Internship (LTI) program, working with a mentor on site. The internship is the core around which each student's personal curriculum is built. Each student meets with a parent, an advisor (teacher), and a mentor to plan the curriculum. A student who is interested in getting into real estate will have to learn math, how to read maps, and people skills; one who wants to build boats must learn math, physics, and carpentry; a student who interns in a restaurant because he wants to become a chef and one day own a restaurant will have to learn chemistry (how heat affects food), nutrition, and business management.

One young woman decided in her first semester that she wanted to be a secretary, so she interned in a physician's office as a file clerk. She became interested in medicine, so her next internship was with a physical therapist; then she spent a semester working in a hospital emergency room. She needed to know science, so The Met arranged for her to take courses at nearby Brown University.

Another student did her LTI with a Providence police officer, and her main project was to help the department improve relations with teenagers. (She also spent time in a squad car and was involved in responses to everything from domestic disputes to homicides.) With help from a Brown University sociologist, she developed a survey and gathered responses from 120 students in high school classrooms. Two of her findings contradicted the police department's prevailing beliefs. First, many students reported positive attitudes toward the police; and second, students reported that their contacts with police occurred more often in schools and community centers than on the streets. Based on these findings, her final report challenged the department's emphasis on community policing as the best way to improve relations with teenagers. She suggested that the police should increase their positive presence in schools and community centers instead.

Met students design projects that let them explore their interests more deeply. For example, two young African American women (sophomores) followed Martin Luther King's footsteps on the 1965 march from Selma to Montgomery. They spent weeks preparing, reading books and contemporary newspapers and magazines. They interviewed people who had participated in the march.

Shortly after they got back to school, they were part of a panel at a meeting at Brown that I attended. I asked them what they had learned. One of them looked me in the eye and said, "The most important thing I learned is that people died so I could vote. I will never ever miss a vote." That is not a lesson that is likely to fade away with the passage of time, nor one that is absorbed so completely by sitting in a civics class.

Another student wrote a play as her senior project. Her advisor and peers urged her to produce it, so she did. She recruited a cast, directed the production, acted in it, and, in addition, she rented a hall, printed the advertising, and sold the tickets to the show. Think about the variety of real situations in which she learned.

To graduate, each Met student must write an autobiography. When Met students receive a degree, their advisors make personal comments about them—like honorary degree citations. At the first commencement ceremony in 1997, the advisor presented the diploma to one student with a comment that went like this: "When Hector came to The Met and learned he'd have to write a 75-page autobiography to graduate, he said he'd never make it—couldn't write and didn't have anything interesting to say. Well, he turned in his autobiography last week; it wasn't 75 pages, it was 100 pages. And he thanked me for making him write it, saying, 'Until I wrote that, I didn't know who I was.'"

Real-Life Learning

Real-life learning gives even younger kids a chance to be creative. A mother volunteered to teach writing to 5th graders in her son's elementary school. She didn't assign essays like "how I spent my summer" but instead encouraged the kids to write about what most interested them. When a youngster couldn't think of anything, she engaged in a conversation that drew out ideas and feelings the student didn't know he had. The results were extraordinary—rich in emotion and imagery. With a sense of excitement and accomplishment, the students read their work for the public at a Borders bookstore one evening.

Sitting in a room with a group of people all the same age listening to a teacher lecture on an academic topic is not a "natural" way of learning. It may work for some college students who are thinking about careers and are highly motivated to learn, and for others if they see the relevance of the subject to the world they live in or to their own lives. In general, however, we tend to learn best when we have a practical reason to.

I hated every minute of my three months of basic training in the Army. I hated the weather, the grueling demands on my body, the humiliation inflicted by what seemed like sadistic drill sergeants. But I learned how to fire my weapon accurately and to field-strip it blindfolded in less than a minute. I learned how to find land mines and disarm them. I learned to navigate unfamiliar terrain using a map and a compass.

Even though the pedagogy consisted of lecturing, drills, and practice, I learned these things for the simple reason that not knowing them could cost me my life. You might say that I was highly motivated, and I still remember much of that stuff decades later.

Elliot Washor, codirector of The Met, writes about a cycle of text to life and life to text. The traditional approach of schools is to rely on the text to prepare students for life—learn academic material in classrooms from lectures and books, then apply the knowledge in real life. Washor argues that learning is far more likely to result if it occurs in real life, which motivates the student to return to the text for more information.

In a 2009 article, Washor and coauthors Charles Mojkowski and Deborah Foster take on the lack of reading proficiency among a majority of America's youth. The popular culture, especially technology and the Internet, are often blamed for the problem. But Washor and his colleagues make the case for "the powerful interchange between young people's experiences in the world and what they read" (p. 521). They argue that experiences "give students the curiosity and motivation to learn more from text and the confidence to pursue their interests. The cycle of experience and reading—a cycle of life to text and text to life—is at the heart of literacy and learning" (p. 521). The article continues:

> The problem is that the life-to-text and text-to-life cycle is not addressed in most schools because it runs counter to the prevailing notions about what should be read, when, and how. By and large, schools ignore the power of students' interests to provide the motivation to read and fail to exploit the experience-to-reading-to-experience cycle. Instead,

schools genuflect to the prescribed canon about what is important to read and when it must be read, thereby reducing the quest for literacy to the conquest of a reading list.

Consequently, many young people come to associate reading with schooling rather than with learning more about what interests them, both in their broad and focused investigations. What schools teach, subliminally if not overtly, about real-world literacy is actually antithetical to what we wish for our young people. It teaches that literacy is about a set of skills, not a way to engage a part of the world that a young person may care about. (p. 522)

The history of experiential learning is long and distinguished, and the philosophy has established beachheads in schools, colleges, and organizations across the world—often in related learning programs like inquiry based, project based, hands-on, cooperative, service, career and technical, and vocational. But real-world learning has never been widely adopted by mainstream education. That situation is especially disturbing because a study done by the Horatio Alger Association of Distinguished Americans (2005) found that 95 percent of students think "more real-world learning would improve their school" (p. 23).

Laura Goldstein, the Brown student who helped me with research for this book, agrees and cites her own teaching experience:

When I was teaching high school English, my students were always wondering how the material we learned in class would serve them in the "real world." The curriculum I was required to teach was narrowly driven by the district's high-stakes testing. When most of what we did in class was in preparation for the test they would take in the spring, I found myself unable to explain to them why the content was relevant to their lives outside of school and the future careers they were aiming for. For most of the year I found myself constantly looking for new ways to engage students in the material the district imposed on us, and constantly felt like I was failing. But then there would come a period of the year post-test, from March until June, when teachers were free to plan field trips and cultural events and shed constraining test preparation from their lesson plans. During this period there was a noticeable rise in student engagement, and questions of "Why are we learning this?" subsided around the building. (Goldstein, 2008)

Real World in the Classroom

Real-life learning doesn't always have to happen outside of school; good teachers can bring it into the classroom.

A small-scale example recently appeared in *Education Week* (Ash, 2009). Purdue University scholars focused on five classes of 8th graders in a rural Indiana school. The students were taught about the effect that humans have on water and water quality. Some of the students "learned" the material through lectures and textbooks, and the rest participated in building a water-purification device as a way of learning the concepts. Students who built the hands-on water-purification system were found to have "a deeper understanding" of the concepts than the students who had lecture-based lessons.

Here's one more close-to-home example of experiential learning taking place when teaching engages students in real-life situations. A few years ago, my daughter Lauren, a writer and editor who had a temporary teacher certification, substituted at a Cape Cod high school. On one occasion the teacher she replaced had to leave suddenly for an emergency and had not left a lesson plan. She had left a note advising her substitute that the class could be used as a study hour.

When Lauren got to the classroom, the 10th graders were shouting, running around the room, and generally raising hell. Suppressing her panic, she shouted louder than they did and finally got them in their seats and reasonably quiet. "I need to ask you for a favor," she said. Taking a manuscript from her briefcase, she explained that it was a draft of a book for teenagers that a publisher had asked her to read and comment on.

"It's been a long time since I was a teenager," she said, "so I would really appreciate it if I could read some parts of the manuscript to you and get your opinion on whether it works." Several students nodded, so Lauren began to read. The students were completely absorbed and silent. She read for about 20 minutes and then asked, "What do you think?"

Several hands shot up. During the next 20 minutes, most of the students offered opinions and ideas, and several times the students eagerly discussed a point among themselves. Lauren later told me that their comments were quite perceptive. "They nailed it," she said.

When the bell rang, the students were noisily talking about the book as they left. One young woman walked up to the desk and quietly said, "I hope you can stay and be our teacher, because that was the best class I ever had."

I think they call that a "teachable moment" in education school. The students were not motivated when they entered the classroom. For any learning to occur, the teacher had to capture their interest or provoke their curiosity. Lauren did that by letting them know she valued their opinions. And they responded because they were asked to do something that they thought was useful and important.

I doubt my daughter had read John Dewey, but she instinctively knew what he would advise: "Give the pupils something to do, not something to learn; and the doing is of such a nature as to demand thinking; learning naturally results" (Dewey, 1916, p. 181).

How is it that despite positive research findings and the testimony of teachers and students, real-world learning is not a significant part of schooling for most of our middle and high school students? The answer, I think, lies in the strong academic culture of schooling and its almost slavish dependence on textbooks and formal instruction. In the past two decades, the situation has worsened. The growing influence of standards-based accountability, the powerful effect of No Child Left Behind, and the persistent pressure to get higher scores on standardized tests leave educators little incentive to venture far from the highly structured school day.

Some years ago, a well-regarded suburban high school instituted the senior year project. The local newspaper published a feature focusing on a young man, interning with the ACLU, who studied the student handbook from school districts in the state to assess whether student rights were being infringed. His research made news. Teachers and administrators in the school praised the program. One teacher said it was the best experience she'd ever had as a teacher.

Later, in an education conference session, two teachers from the school proudly described the project.

"So you're saying it was really successful?" I asked.

"Absolutely!"

"Then I assume you will add a junior year project."

The teachers looked stunned. "Are you kidding?" one asked. "There simply isn't room in the curriculum. We were barely able to do the senior project."

I am always amazed at how often in education the status quo is snatched from the jaws of innovation. A program thought to be highly successful by students, teachers, and parents is considered a dispensable add-on to the deeply entrenched curriculum.

A bright, articulate 11th grader summed it up for me some years ago when I asked how he was doing in his "good" suburban high school. He frowned, hesitated, then replied that he and many of his friends really hated it and couldn't wait to get out.

I asked him why.

He shrugged, thought for a moment, and then replied, "It's like school gets in the way of life."

A new-schools strategy would encourage schools to make real-world education the dominant form of pedagogy.

| CHAPTER 14 |

It's the Work That Counts

ASSUMPTION: *Student assessment based on multiple measures, focusing mainly on the student's actual work, is a better and fairer way to evaluate student performance than standardized tests.*

Back in the mid-1990s I saw an animated film produced by students in a media program in a California high school. I think it was called *The Red Bicycle*, and it made an enduring impression on me.

The film opens with a teacher lecturing her class on how to ride a bicycle. She has a chart of bicycle parts in the front of the room and is droning on about how they work and how one should proceed to ride. One lad in the back of the room is gazing out an open window and sees a bike leaning against a tree. With the teacher's back turned, he slips out and gets on the bicycle and wobbles away. Ten minutes later, he pedals smoothly back, returns the bike, and slips back into the classroom just in time to take a test the teacher is about to hand out.

Because he missed a crucial part of her lecture about how to ride a bike, he fails the test. But when the teacher takes the class outside to ride the red bicycle, he is the only student who pedals away with no problems.

These students saw the obvious disconnect between a written test and actual performance in demonstrating proficiency. I remember thinking, if only our education decision makers were as insightful.

Recently a group of prominent educators provided some high-powered decision makers with such insights. They met with leaders of the National Governors Association (NGA) and the Council of Chief State School Officers (CCSSO)—the main proponents of common standards and a national curriculum—along with officials from the U.S. Department of Education, which will award grants of $350 million to develop new standardized tests closely linked to the common standards. Armed with a major paper by Stanford University professor Linda Darling-Hammond, the panel urged the decision makers to move away from standardized multiple-choice tests, which at best provide a snapshot of student performance at a particular time, to deeper, more analytical assessments, tasks, and projects that require students to solve and discuss complex problems. Ms. Hammond outlined a comprehensive system that includes summative and formative tests of higher-order thinking skills that are increasingly needed in the modern workplace.

Maybe they made some progress. According to a story in *Education Week* (Gewertz, 2010) describing the meeting, Gene Wilhoit, the CCSSO's executive director, said common standards must be accompanied by improved assessment, new types of curriculum, and better teacher preparation and professional development. And Dane Linn, who oversees the common-standards work for the NGA, said a vital part of next-generation assessments is the role they must play in learning. "The assessments we end up with have to inform instruction," he said. If they don't change educators' practice, he said, "then what good are they?" (Gewertz, 2010, "Common Standards," para. 3).

Both statements are correct. The question is whether authentic, performance-based assessments are compatible with common standards and a common curriculum.

The Essential Role of Performance Assessments

In a new-schools strategy of education improvement, performance assessments are not only compatible with personalized education, they are inextricably linked. I don't believe one works without the other.

Although formative testing by teachers and end-of-course examinations are valid measures of student progress, the almost total reliance on standardized test scores to assess students is impeding learning and distorting the educational process. Its primary purpose is accountability, not measurement of a student's learning or progress toward learning goals. Yet standardized testing has an enormous effect on what takes place in the classroom.

As adults, we are almost never evaluated mainly on the basis of test scores. Our performance is assessed on several measures—the work we produce, our skills, our attitudes and behavior, our ability to work in teams and deal with others.

Only in extracurricular activities do most schools evaluate students on their performance—how well they sing, or march in the band, or argue in the debate, or act on the stage, or work with others in team efforts. Who would asses a student's ability to play the piano using a paper-and-pencil test?

Why shouldn't mastery of academic content also be judged on actual work—portfolios of a semester's assignments, exhibitions and presentations, recitals, science projects, research papers, off-campus service work, and internships? Why shouldn't schools use such multiple measures to evaluate students?

The main reason offered is the psychometricians' insistence that most of the multiple measures lack objectivity, that they rely on human judgment rather than data that can be quantified. It's true that performance assessment is subjective, but so are the measures used to evaluate most of us in our adult work and behavior. How many of us in the workplace have not sat through performance reviews with our supervisor to be rated according to his or her *opinion* of how we performed?

Authentic evaluation of students is not simply based on feeling or the mood a teacher happens to be in. As part of a well-constructed performance-based assessment system, teachers use rubrics or criteria to assess performance—which they often help develop—not unlike those used in Olympic competitions to judge the performance of some athletes, including divers, gymnasts, and skaters.

Teachers work together to judge the quality of student work, to determine, for example, whether a piece of writing is excellent, average, or poor. They can judge the arts that way, and public speaking. Such rubrics are indeed subjective measures, because "objective" tests are not useful in evaluating genuine learning any more than they are in assessing the football player, the pianist, the singer, the debater, or the writer.

Assessment Linked to Teaching

What teachers learn from observing and rating student performance is directly related to teaching: how well the students have or have not learned the material and where further work is most needed. In short, performance-based systems closely tie learning to instruction and evaluation to teaching, and they encourage teachers to think deeply about what constitutes good, average, and poor performance.

Moreover, performance tasks foster collaborative relationships between teachers and students in which the teacher describes the standards and requirements and the student may choose the means of demonstrating mastery. The result is usually a richer and deeper connection between teachers and students.

In a performance assessment system that requires students to produce evidence that they understand the content and can apply it in what are often called real-world situations, they also participate in evaluating themselves. They are often required to reflect on their own work and to judge their own performance. Interestingly, it is common for students to be more critical of themselves than their teachers are of them.

Ann Cook, codirector of Urban Academy, an alternative school in New York City, is a feisty opponent of standardized tests and a passionate supporter of performance assessments. She is also cochair of the New York Performance Standards Consortium, which has about 30 member schools across the state and advocates for performance assessment.

Her students at Urban Academy develop skills in courses that include projects, papers, exhibits, presentations, and experiments through which students demonstrate proficiency in six academic areas: literature, mathematics, social studies, science, creative arts, and art criticism. To earn their diplomas, students must show proficiency in these subjects, pass required courses, and be competent in library research and computer use. They must also show continual progress in the areas of community service, contribution to the Urban Academy community, class participation, and independent reading.

In one outstanding instance, a young woman demonstrated her proficiency in creative arts proficiency by making *A Girl Like Me*—a film that portrays the experiences of black girls whom she interviewed about their experiences (Holland & Evans, 2006). The film won numerous awards and was selected for the 2006 Tribeca Film Festival.

Performance-based assessments are the logical extension of personalized education because students are encouraged to pursue their own interests and are thus judged on their individual performance. When required to be active participants in learning rather than passive receptacles of facts, students become engaged in gathering information, analyzing it, evaluating it, relating it, and applying it. By having to carry out tasks in the context of a curriculum tied to state standards, students must organize the information around major disciplinary concepts, thus enhancing their learning and understanding.

When standards are flexible and concentrate on the organizing concepts of a discipline, performance assessment of a student's work can focus on how the work is linked to curricula and state standards. When students do well in performance assessments, they demonstrate that they have learned both the material and how to use it. In short, the assessment is in itself a form of teaching and learning.

In the fall of 2006, I was asked to serve as a recorder of a two-day conference in Manchester hosted by the state of New Hampshire. Representatives from six other states—Arizona, Kansas, Maine, Oregon, Rhode Island, and Washington—participated in the meeting to discuss whether "Performance Assessments Can Transform the American High School."

Do Two States Make a Trend?

Rhode Island and New Hampshire began their journey to performance assessments in the late 1990s. Rhode Island's new diploma requirements became effective with the graduating class of 2008; New Hampshire's program became fully effective with the class of 2009.

The New Hampshire and Rhode Island systems have much in common but also differ in specific detail. Together, they embody the essential elements of a comprehensive performance- or competency-based system. (Detailed information about the provisions described here can be found on the websites of the two state departments of education. For New Hampshire, see http://www.education.nh.gov/index.htm; for Rhode Island, see http://www.ride.ri.gov.)

- **Personalized Education.** Both systems encourage students to "pursue their interests and passions both inside and outside of school." The Rhode Island Diploma System states: "Whether a student is interested in rock music, sports, cooking, car mechanics, or fashion design, most passions can reasonably become a subject for a demonstration of proficiency in content and applied skills" (McWalters, 2005, p. 5). New Hampshire encourages personalized learning, focusing on Commissioner Lyonel Tracy's Follow the Child initiative (New Hampshire Department of Education, 2010), in which educators collect data related to students and follow their developmental, personal, social, physical, and academic progress over time, seeking to ensure that each student succeeds in school and beyond.
- **Multiple Assessments.** Using several metrics to assess students is an indispensable part of a competency-based system. In Rhode Island, schools choose at least two of four options: digital portfolio, exhibition, certificate of initial mastery, or end-of-course examinations. New Hampshire schools are responsible for choosing how they will assess performance but are encouraged by the state to think of assessments "as extending beyond a single test to multiple" measures, which include formative tests to diagnose individual student achievement.
- **Course Requirements.** Students must still take and pass courses in core academic subjects aligned with state standards. But the courses have been redesigned from content-heavy, traditional, top-down instruction to be competency-based. New Hampshire became the first state to regulate the elimination of the Carnegie unit—that arcane

measure that awards credit for hours of seat time in a course. Instead, student achievement will be assessed through a demonstration of mastery of the material in the course and the ability to apply it. Rhode Island retains the term "Carnegie units," but it now applies to courses that are based on competence rather than seat time.

- **Competencies.** In addition to acquiring knowledge in the five disciplines of English language arts, mathematics, science, social studies, and the arts, New Hampshire has developed the following competencies to be demonstrated: problem solving and decision making, self-management, communication skills, ability to work with others, and information use (such as research, analysis, and technology). New Hampshire's performance assessment of course competencies applies to all high school courses, as well as any "extended learning opportunities" in which learning is to be granted credit toward graduation.

  To the required five academic competencies, Rhode Island adds technology and applied learning standards (which include critical thinking and problem solving, decision making, research and analytic reasoning, and personal or social responsibility). Rhode Island students also must complete two schoolwide diploma assessments (exhibitions, portfolios, or end-of-course exams).

- **Statewide Examinations.** In addition to performance assessments, New Hampshire students must also participate in the statewide exams in English language arts, mathematics, and (starting in 2008) science, but a student's graduation is not dependent on the state test scores. Rather, credit toward graduation is earned through the demonstration of mastery of course competencies. In Rhode Island, all students must participate in statewide exams in English language arts, mathematics, and science. State exam scores at first could not count for more than 10 percent of the overall determination of proficiency for graduation, but that was subsequently raised to 30 percent, and students must now complete 20 credits' worth of classes; submit a senior project or portfolio;

and score at least "partially proficient" on standardized tests in English and math in order to graduate.

- **Real-World Learning.** New Hampshire's program of extended learning opportunities lets students pursue alternative approaches outside of the classroom to acquire knowledge and skills. The program reinforces the concept of learning "any time, any place" as long as the learning opportunity is an experience that meets the same quality standard of the classroom and is "rigorous and relevant to the student, and is personalized"—that is, connecting the student, teacher, and community in an authentic way. The Rhode Island Diploma System "certifies proficiency in content knowledge as well as the ability to apply that knowledge to real-world projects and problems."

The Rigor of Performance Assessments

Some skeptics worry that performance assessments are not "rigorous" (one of the most overused and misused words in education) and involve only "soft" skills. Visit any school with performance assessments and learn otherwise.

Ann Cook's New York Performance Standards Consortium lists four competencies that a good performance system should measure in the form of culminating projects at the high school level: literary analysis, mathematical problem solving, original science experiments, and research in social studies demonstrating the use of argument and evidence (Schmoker, 2008/2009).

The rigor of the work is evident in the titles of some of the projects, such as "Why Do They Have to Die? A Comparative Analysis of the Protagonists' Deaths in *Dr. Jekyll and Mr. Hyde*" and "Finding the Parabolic Path of a Comet as It Moves Through the Solar System." Other projects have involved conducting an experiment to determine what combination of focal length and aperture of a pinhole camera creates the best image, and writing a research paper on the meaning of the "free exercise" clause in the First Amendment.

No state has been using performance assessments long enough to accumulate a persuasive record of success, but New Hampshire can provide some limited and encouraging indicators of success drawn from the experience of four schools that participated in a pilot program of competency-based assessment.

The results were very positive, with high levels of performance for almost all indicators. An article in *Education Week* quotes a report on the project, saying, "While there is some year-to-year variation, as is to be expected, the data demonstrate a clear trend that more students are staying in high school, more students are graduating from high school, more students are better prepared for success beyond high school, and more students are planning to go on to postsecondary education" (DiMartino, 2007, para. 18). Over the five-year period studied, the dropout rate was cut in half in two of the schools and improved in a third.

The trend also showed improvement in SAT combined verbal and math scores and in the scores on the state's English language arts and mathematics assessments. All four schools showed improvement in language arts, and three schools showed improvement in mathematics. A general trend showed an increase in the number of students scoring "advanced" or "proficient," the two highest categories, and an equally important reduction in the percentage scoring "novice," the lowest of the categories. All four schools exceeded the state average for the percentage of students scoring advanced or proficient in language arts, and two were above the state average in mathematics. These improved scores on standardized tests are meaningful because they are the result of true mastery of information, not simply memorization of factoids.

Based on the New Hampshire pilot and the limited use of performance assessments elsewhere, there is reason to believe that they can produce significant benefits, such as the following:

- Better student attendance, fewer dropouts, and higher graduation rates
- Increased student motivation
- Higher student and teacher morale
- Demonstrations of high performance and mastery in courses
- High-quality student work
- Enthusiastic participation in out-of-school learning projects

- Higher college attendance rates, lower remediation rates, and higher college completion rates
- Successful school-to-work transitions
- Higher scores on standardized tests

Given the promise, why don't more states and districts turn to performance-based assessments?

Because they represent a profound departure from what educators have been doing for a century, the new requirements for graduation in New Hampshire and Rhode Island were phased in over almost a decade. In Rhode Island, superintendents and principals were dragged kicking and screaming into the new system. New Hampshire schools were largely negative toward the move.

Teachers are initially wary of performance assessments because they take more time and effort than correcting a multiple-choice test and coming up with a score. Performance evaluation means teachers must become more deeply engaged in the students' work and must be willing to personalize their instruction.

Some parents in both states were upset because they could no longer rely conveniently and completely on simple letter grades and test scores to judge their kids' performance and compare them to other students. I have always been somewhat mystified that parents would rather have their child's performance expressed in an *A* or a *C* than in a written evaluation of the student's work and behavior. Of course, a letter grade satisfies parents' need to compare their child with other children, which is even more unfathomable—especially since the value of letter grades varies greatly from teacher to teacher.

Although not a lot of hard data are available on the costs of performance-based assessments, it is likely that they cost more than standardized testing. But a significant part of that increased cost is in supporting the collaboration among teachers and students to produce and fairly evaluate real work.

Although New Hampshire and Rhode Island are pushing ahead with reasonable success, the culture and practices of the existing system are so deeply embedded that I find it hard to believe that performance-based assessments will ever be widely adopted by conventional schools. We have an assessment system that can be used to compare and hold schools and students accountable, but it is a lousy measure of real learning and personal growth. We need an assessment system that demonstrates student mastery and encourages good habits of mind and behavior even though it is not as useful for comparison and accountability.

For the good of the society and the rising generations of young people, leaders must find the imagination and flexibility to use different instruments to accomplish both important goals.

| CHAPTER 15 |

Start Them Early

ASSUMPTION: *High-quality preschool programs and good elementary schools lay the foundation for educational success by stimulating students' curiosity and providing them with the basic skills they need to succeed in later years.*

As I pointed out in the Introduction, approximately 25 of every 100 students drop out before graduating (Stillwell, 2010), and only 24 percent of high schoolers who took the ACT were college-ready in all subject areas. In fall 2000, 28 percent of entering college freshmen enrolled in one or more remedial reading, writing, or mathematics courses (Parsad & Lewis, 2003).

The message of those few statistics is that the majority of the young people who enroll in our public schools are poorly served—they either drop out or get a diploma but are not adequately prepared for college or work.

This failure has multiple causes. Some of them are socioeconomic and cultural factors that cannot be remedied by simply improving education. But education can make an enormous contribution to a long-term solution by providing high-quality preschool learning opportunities to every child beginning at age 3 or 4 and by improving elementary schools to ensure that every child learns to read, speak, listen, and do arithmetic proficiently.

Despite a growing body of evidence to the contrary, we tend to underestimate the brainpower of preschool children. Anecdotal and scientific research shows that children begin to learn at birth and, under the right conditions, become steadily more proficient learners as they reach school age.

Children are naturally curious, intrigued by the world around them. By the time they are 3 they are capable of learning the rudiments of reading, writing, and arithmetic. In his book *The Unschooled Mind: How Children Think and How Schools Should Teach*, Harvard psychologist and educator Howard Gardner (1993) writes that by the time children are 5 years old they have, among other accomplishments, mastered complex languages, developed number skills, begun to build a framework of ethical behavior, and developed plausible theories about people and the world.

Brain Studies Point the Way

I don't know much about the physiology of the brain or specifically how it is involved in learning or memory. I know enough to be very skeptical of commercial programs on the market that claim to be based on brain research. But if I were an educator working with students and curricula, I'd know more and I would ponder how that knowledge could improve my practice.

Studies of how we learn and how our brain works have multiplied significantly over the past few decades. One doesn't have to be a neuroscientist to glean from them what is useful. For instance, the *New York Times* recently published "Studying Young Minds, and How to Teach Them," summarizing some of the research under way by cognitive scientists to better understand the relationship of the brain to learning and schooling, particularly regarding the learning of mathematics (Carey, 2009). At a number of universities—Buffalo, Harvard, Carnegie Mellon, Clark, and the Collège de France in Paris, for example—researchers are finding that children have at least a rudimentary understanding of reading, language, arithmetic, and even geometry as early as age 4.

Using imaging technology, scientists can observe the brain at work as students participate in different activities. They have discovered that a particular section of the brain (the parietal cortex) near the temple lights up when children are trying to calculate quantities. It appears that when children see specific quantities, neurons in this area respond. When students "interact" with numbers and quantities, these regions fire neurons in the frontal lobe where reasoning occurs.

Such findings are leading to the development of new ways of teaching math that are proving to be more effective than traditional curricula. One example comes from researcher Julie Sarama and her husband, Professor Doug Clements, both in the graduate school of education at the University of Buffalo. Together they have developed Building Blocks, a program designed to facilitate math education in preschool children. The *Times* article describes it this way:

> In a Building Blocks classroom, numbers are in artwork, on computer games, and in lessons, sharing equal time with letters. Like "Sesame Street," Building Blocks has children play creative counting games; but it also focuses on other number skills, including cardinality (how many objects are in a set) and one-to-one correspondence (matching groups of objects, like cups and saucers). Teachers can tailor the Building Blocks lesson to a student's individual ability. (Carey, 2009, "Beyond Counting," para. 5)

Testing of students in more than 400 classrooms showed that those in Building Blocks made considerably more progress than students not in the program. After one school year, children in the program scored in the 76th percentile on average on tests of addition, subtraction, and number recognition compared with children in other classrooms who scored in the 50th percentile. Moreover, Building Blocks students retained what they learned, ranking in the 71st percentile a year after the program ended.

In addition to academic learning, research is looking at the brain's effect on behavior. Some schools, for example, are now using a program based on brain research to aid the development of the frontal lobe in preschool students to improve self-control in the classroom.

Even before brain research had much influence on pedagogy and curricular decisions, the case for early education was effectively made by a number of longitudinal studies (the most reliable education research), beginning with the High Scope/Perry Preschool study, which followed 123 African American children for more than 40 years (Schweinhart et al., 2005). These studies show that children who attended preschool did much better as they matured than those who didn't. They were significantly more likely to do better academically and graduate; less likely to need special-needs services, to drop out of school, and to become involved with the criminal justice system; and more likely to get a higher-paying job and to be employed full time.

The Promising Results of Preschool

Surveys of preschool programs in Chicago, Michigan, North Carolina, and Maryland show the same benefits of those in the Perry study, as noted in these results gathered by an advocacy organization called Pre-K Now (n.d.):

- Children who attended a pre-K program in Chicago were 29 percent more likely to graduate from high school than their peers who did not have pre-K.
- Maryland 5th graders who attended pre-K were 44 percent less likely to have repeated a grade than their peers who did not attend pre-K.
- Chicago children who attended pre-K were less likely to require special education services than their peers who did not attend.
- Chicago children who did not attend pre-K were 70 percent more likely to be arrested for a violent crime by age 18 than their peers who had been pre-K participants.
- North Carolina children who attended pre-K were less likely to become teen parents than their peers who did not attend pre-K (26 percent versus 45 percent).
- Forty-year-old adults in Michigan who attended pre-K as children were more likely to be employed and had a 33 percent higher average income than their peers who did not have pre-K.

This persuasive evidence has led to increasing participation in preschool for children from middle- and upper-income families. Preschool programs now exist in 38 states. Nationally, 66 percent of 4-year-olds and more than 40 percent of 3-year-olds were enrolled in a preschool education program in 2005 (NIEER, 2007). But many of the neediest children do not attend preschool programs.

James Heckman, a Nobel Prize–winning economist at the University of Chicago, has estimated that for every dollar spent on a prekindergarten like Perry, $8 has been gained in higher incomes for participants and in savings on the costs related to extra schooling, crime, and welfare. In a 2009 paper on the rate of return of the Perry program, Heckman and colleagues acknowledged various shortcomings in his earlier research and concluded that the rate of return is substantially lower than the previously estimated 16 percent; his latest estimate puts the rate at closer to 6 percent.

Early education is especially important for children who live in poverty or with one parent who probably didn't graduate from high school. Research shows that an average child from a lower-socioeconomic-status home starts kindergarten with an average vocabulary of 3,000 words, while the child from a middle-class home starts with an average vocabulary of 20,000 words (Hart & Risley, 1995). Children cannot learn words that they do not hear.

Disadvantaged children arrive at 1st grade woefully unprepared to learn. Without early intervention, one study projected, only about two in five boys would graduate from high school, fewer than 5 percent would enroll in college, and more than 40 percent would wind up convicted of crimes or on probation (Heckman, 2007). Boys who participated in a preschool program were more likely to earn a high school diploma and attend college. They were also considerably less likely to be convicted of crimes or go on welfare.

We have made a good start on universal preschool education, but we have a lot of work to do to fund it adequately, provide well-trained teachers, and make sure the parents of the neediest children understand the programs and take advantage of them. And we must ensure that they are based on the best research and observational data available.

The Importance of Play

In typical fashion, professional educators and policymakers have already begun to push for "rigorous" curricula and testing in kindergarten and preschool. A major report by the Alliance for Childhood begins this way:

> The argument of this report, that child-initiated play must be restored to kindergarten, will be dismissed and even ridiculed in some quarters. In spite of the fact that the vital importance of play in young children's development has been shown in study after study, many people believe that play is a waste of time in school. School, they say, should be a place for learning. There's plenty of time for play at home. (Miller & Almon, 2009, p. 7)

But, as the report notes, "Research shows that children who engage in complex forms of socio-dramatic play have greater language skills than nonplayers, better social skills, more empathy, more imagination, and more of the subtle capacity to know what others mean. They are less aggressive and show more self-control and higher levels of thinking" (p. 7).

What is so often forgotten in conventional schools (if it was ever believed) is that learning should be fun and not stressful. How can anyone who watches children explore, discover, and create not be convinced of this? Children at play immerse themselves in what they are doing. They are self-motivated. They are in "the zone." Mihaly Csikszentmihalyi, in his book *Flow* (1990), argues that people are most happy when they are in a state of flow—completely absorbed by the activity they are engaged in. Childhood play fosters one's ability to control the flow of experience and thus promote happiness. It nourishes the imagination and unleashes hidden potential.

Sir Ken Robinson (2005), the internationally recognized leader in the study of the development of innovation and creativity, challenges the way we're educating our children. He tells the story of a girl sitting at the back of the classroom unengaged in the lesson. One day the teacher comes up behind her and sees that she is drawing.

"What are you drawing?" the teacher asks sternly.

"I'm drawing a picture of God," says the girl.

The teacher rebukes her, declaring that no one knows what God looks like.

"Well," the girl says, "they will when I'm finished."

That anecdote captures the natural imagination of a child, and we should take pains to nourish it whenever we can.

The Need to Reorganize School

Establishing the best universal preschools and kindergartens possible will be painfully insufficient if we do not change elementary schools to build on that early progress.

Teachers and researchers will testify that students learn in different ways and at different speeds, and that some successfully complete their work much more quickly than others. Different students process information differently; we all do. Some are very sequential and well organized in their approach; others are more random. These varieties present an instructional challenge for teachers. If the teacher gears instruction to the students in the class who learn quickly, the slower students fall further and further behind; if the teacher adapts the instruction to serve the slower students, the faster-learning students get bored. In part, that is why the nefarious practice of tracking was instituted.

While it is not as orderly and requires more personal attention from teachers, a more rational school would eliminate grade levels as such and group students for varying periods of time according to what they are expected to master (much as was the custom in the one-room schoolhouse). Schools have been experimenting with clustering students on some other basis than chronological age, but the vast majority of schools operate on the age/grade basis.

When the current standards-based reform strategy was launched in the late 1980s, one of its main provisions was that students who needed more time to master the standards should get it. Students who master the standards more quickly than expected should advance.

Some school districts in Alaska have allowed students to move ahead when they demonstrate proficiency, but until 2008 they had no followers. In 2008, the Adams 50 district, serving a working-class suburb north of Denver, decided to eliminate grade levels and instead group students based on what they know. The district has 10,000 students and 21 schools. Seventy-two percent of its students qualify for federal meal benefits, two-thirds are Latino, and 38 percent are learning English. The district had been put on academic watch because only 60 percent of its students graduate on time.

According to an article in the *Denver Post*, Superintendent Roberta Selleck concluded that the policy that led to the "academic watch" status was not working and a change was necessary. Commenting on the new reform strategy, she said, "In a standards-based system, time becomes the variable and learning is the constant. . . . Learning becomes much more 24-7" (Meyer, 2008, para. 10).

Changing the way elementary schools operate is especially crucial to build on the gains of preschool education. As argued earlier, the main goal of elementary school should be to teach children the basics of reading, writing, and arithmetic. The goal is to develop the basic skills of literacy so that students are reading proficiently for comprehension ideally by age 9, but at least by age 11. Failure to accomplish this goal almost guarantees that students will struggle when they enter middle school and begin to deal with abstract concepts.

I remember in a 7th grade geography class being asked to list the principal products of Peru. Many kids, especially those who are disadvantaged, would interpret that as "the blah blah of blah." Critics argue that this is because they have not acquired the knowledge, and skill can't be learned except in a context of knowledge. That is true. Basal readers are rightfully rejected because they do not provide a context of real content. One cannot learn skills without a context of knowledge, but in the elementary school, the emphasis should be on the skill.

I would argue that reading and writing should not be taught simply as the skill to decode, but instead should be taught in subject-matter context. Students should learn to read by reading literature and stories about history, geography, and science. And they should learn their skills through hands-on activities and field trips into the real world.

As students enter middle school, beginning at age 12, the emphasis should shift increasingly to knowledge. Students who are proficient in reading and writing are prepared to master the subject matter in the various disciplines.

Reorganizing the educational system for children ages 3 and 4 in preschool, age 5 in kindergarten, and ages 6–10 in elementary school, may well—indeed, should—lead to major structural changes in middle school and high school. A case can be made that middle school should not have grades but should include children ages 11 and 12. Emphasis should be on the acquisition of knowledge, but students should be able to shape what they study so it is compatible with their interests. Students would be encouraged and guided by their advisor/teachers to take more responsibility for their own education.

At the final stage of the precollegiate educational spectrum, youngsters in secondary school should be expected to be more independent and be able to choose among a number of different education pathways. They should have the opportunity to pursue more deeply a route that develops more fully the skills and knowledge they will need when they leave public school.

Adding two preschool years at the beginning of the educational process, personalizing education, and restructuring elementary and middle school should enable a youngster to accomplish in 10 additional years after kindergarten what now requires 12 more years. Students should receive a diploma by age 16 and be ready for postsecondary education or the workforce, or to pursue an alternative path like the military, volunteer service, or continued independent study.

High School: The Special Problem

The notion of ending high school after the traditional 10th grade may seem radical, but the problems of the American high school are beyond dispute. Educational historian Larry Cremin (1976) wrote about the crisis of the American high school, asserting that it

> has managed increasingly to isolate young people from the rest of society, organizing them into rigidly defined age groups (freshmen, sophomores, juniors, and seniors) that have little contact with either younger children or adults. . . . [As a result the] ordinary processes of socialization have been weakened, confused, and disjointed; and the symptoms are everywhere apparent—in the steady decline of academic standards in inner-city schools, in the growing irregularity of attendance at most schools, and in the rising incidence of theft, vandalism, personal assault, and general alienation in all schools.

The reorganization I propose would still require students to spend 13 years in formal schooling, but they would start and finish earlier. Simply requiring students to spend more time in our existing education system will not improve their achievement, but if we "do it right" through age 16, they will continue to educate themselves for the rest of their lives.

The idea of starting school earlier and finishing it two years earlier is not a new idea. The California Business Roundtable proposed it in the late 1980s. It didn't get anywhere. Nearly 30 years later, it is still a good idea and worth trying at least on a pilot basis.

We shouldn't stop our restructuring with high school. Harold Hodgkinson (1999), the researcher and scholar who awakened education to its demographic destiny with his Paul Revere–like crisscrossing of America, used to talk about "all one system." In essays and speeches he argued that dividing education into elementary, middle, secondary, and college education made no sense and hampered the process.

Education should be all one system, seamless and integrated. Students would progress through it without the jarring transitions that now exist. Many states now have K–16 commissions to accomplish that goal, but they have a long way to go. According to one report a few years ago, the biggest barrier to their progress is their own structures and policies.

Pursuing a second, parallel strategy of creating new innovative schools would give us the opportunity to expand early education and experiment with new structures and new ideas in our education system.

| CHAPTER 16 |

A New Role for Teachers

ASSUMPTION: *We are more likely to get effective teachers if we educate them differently and modify their traditional role as instructors.*

The current strategy of the standards-based accountability movement puts high-quality teachers at the center of its efforts. Teachers are just as crucial—perhaps more so—in the alternative new-schools strategy, but in significantly different ways.

In middle and high schools that personalize education, teachers are advisors rather than instructors. Instead of lecturing groups of students in classrooms on specific academic topics, advisors help students manage their own education. They also serve as tutors to individual and small groups of students by providing "just in time" instruction. For example, a group of students who are aspiring entrepreneurs find that they need to know how to develop a budget or put together a PowerPoint presentation. So an advisor works with them at that point to learn how to do that.

Most of the innovative new schools I have visited or know about have advisors (although some still call them teachers). The advisor's role includes the duties of both the teacher and the guidance counselor in a conventional school. At The Met, which I know best, each advisor has about 15 students who stay with him or her for the four high school years.

Smallness and closeness foster the relationships between advisor and students that are so crucial to learning. These schools of human scale also encourage relationships between students and students, and among advisors.

Because they work closely with each of their students every day, advisors get to know the students' parents or other primary caregivers, who serve on school committees, help their children develop their individualized learning plans, and attend their exhibitions. Advisors partner with mentors who are supervising their students in out-of-school internships. And they work with each other—sharing information, seeking and giving help, and collaborating to create a healthy culture in the school.

Commonly, advisors and students meet in an "advisory" at the beginning of each day (akin to the homeroom in conventional schools). They discuss what is uppermost on students' minds. One student may relate a recent experience, another may seek advice from his fellow students on a problem, and a third may recruit peers to help with a project. Because they monitor their students' work and progress daily, advisors quickly spot problems and weaknesses. So an advisor might spend time for a few mornings on math problems or writing. Schools also may hold another advisory in the afternoon.

Between advisories, students work on their own or in small groups. They keep day planners, which advisors check regularly to make sure students are scheduling their time and work appropriately. And when necessary, advisors push students who are procrastinating or counsel students who are struggling with problems at home. Notwithstanding the close relationships, good advisors do not overlook missed deadlines, sloppy work, or poor behavior. But they deal with such problems in the spirit of a family rather than a bureaucracy.

The Power of Close Relationships

These close relationships and open, continuous communication help to create a sense of belonging in students and a kind of team spirit in the advisory. And research shows that these have a positive effect on learning. A study at the University of Rhode Island, for example, found that personalization and a sense of belonging correlate with such positive educational and behavioral outcomes as better grades, higher motivation, and graduation rates (Meloro, 2005). And the best predictor of school belonging is the advisor-student relationship.

Because the role of the advisor in the small personalized school is so different from that of the teacher in the conventional school, the question arises whether preparation programs should be different. I don't presume to know what should constitute the ideal preparation of the traditional teacher or the new advisor. But I firmly believe that both should participate in a good liberal arts program and concentrate in a specific discipline. And both should spend at least a year in a postgraduate internship that places them in traditional schools and personalized schools, under the supervision of good, experienced teachers and advisors.

Our education system puts high value on academic specialization. It expects that the teacher who aspires to teach math or history or science will have a college major in the corresponding discipline. A body of research shows that students of teachers who are experts in their discipline learn more than students in the classrooms of teachers who did not major in that discipline. And, indeed, the current school reform movement has tightened requirements that teachers specialize in the discipline they teach.

Every prospective teacher should concentrate in a specific academic subject in college and become as expert in it as possible. But the reason is not to accumulate a vast and specific body of knowledge, but rather to understand the major ideas and concepts in that discipline and how it connects to other disciplines and to real life. Given the rapid expansion of knowledge and the time demands that teachers face, it is highly probable that many will not be able to keep up with the new developments in their discipline. This is a problem not only in science but also in all disciplines, although perhaps to a lesser degree. As noted earlier, history is made and reinterpreted every day, nations come and go, boundaries are constantly changing, and social issues are in continuous flux. High-quality teachers, whatever their specialty, have to be continuous learners, just as they expect their students to be.

AFT founder Al Shanker used to say, only half joking, that the teacher just has to know more than the students and keep ahead of them. That is probably truer when students plan and follow their own curriculum. In personalized education, it is important for advisors to be generalists, to have adequate knowledge of several fields and be able to help students learn what they need and want to learn. It does not denigrate the importance of knowledge to say that education works best when teachers and students learn together. If teachers don't learn, the saying goes, students won't learn.

Teachers' Need for Real-World Learning

Book learning will not suffice for today's teachers. Like the students they will teach, they need to learn in the real world, on site from observation and experience.

Nearly all prospective teachers get some clinical experience during their undergraduate years when they engage in "practice teaching" in a school, under the supervision of an experienced teacher. But practice teaching varies widely in quality (depending on the supervising teacher) and time spent (from a semester or longer to eight weeks or less). For clinical experience to add real value to the prospective teacher's education, the supervising teacher should be highly qualified and a good mentor who is willing to give the students real responsibility and provide ongoing feedback on their performance.

Teaching is as complex and difficult a job as that of a physician or a lawyer. Neither 8 weeks nor 12 weeks of field training in college is enough. A yearlong internship in a clinical situation, like that of a medical student, should be the keystone of teacher preparation, whether the novices intend to teach in a conventional school or a small learning community.

During the course of the internship, student teachers should be supervised by more than one senior teacher (ideally at least one of those teachers should be certified by the National Board for Professional Teaching Standards); they should be exposed to different school cultures and work closely with students in and out of class; and they should participate in the life of the school. The goal of such a clinical experience is to expose practice teachers to the real world of schooling and give them an opportunity to apply (and expand) what they've learned in college.

In a discussion about the teacher as advisor, a friend worried that it would be too much to ask teacher education programs to prepare students for two different roles. The more I think about that, the more I believe that all teachers should be prepared for the role of advisor. A liberal arts education, a concentration in an academic discipline, and an extended and intense clinical relationship would benefit them and their students no matter what kind of school they worked in. And so would the elimination of the low-level, low-standards parts of a teacher preparation program that have been so roundly condemned over the years.

For me, a more serious concern is finding enough teachers who are qualified to work as advisors and who can adjust to an educational environment that does not include the traditional routines of courses and classes, constant testing, letter grades, and the other conventions that now prevail in public schools. In addition, by taking responsibility for individual students in close relationships, advisors inevitably become involved in the personal and emotional problems of their students. That, plus the unpredictability of their long workdays, probably increases stress and eventual burnout.

On the other hand, a Public Agenda poll asked teachers how interested they would be "in working at a charter school that was run and managed by teachers themselves." Some 65 percent of new teachers said they would be very or somewhat interested, but somewhat surprising to me was that half of teachers with 20 years experience said they would be interested (Farkas, Johnson, & Duffett, 2003).

Teachers as Owners

The role of teachers in the future should change in another very important way. As professionals they should have more responsibility for, and influence on, their schools. Unprecedented steps toward that goal were taken in Minnesota in 1994.

First, after a protracted struggle and official opposition, Minnesota New Country (Charter) School received approval to open in rural Henderson. Before the school opened, Ted Kolderie, then at the Humphrey Institute for Public Affairs at the University of Minnesota Center for Policy Studies (now Education Evolving, of St. Paul), approached Dee Thomas, a founder of the school, with a bold, innovative idea. He asked, "What if you didn't have employees? What if you owned the enterprise as a professional practice, much like a law firm or medical practice?" Instead of the traditional model of teachers as employees of a school district with little or no influence on school decision making, Kolderie said, perhaps teachers should form cooperatives and contract their services to schools (Thomas, 2007).

After much debate and legal advice, Thomas persuaded her dubious colleagues at New Country to try Kolderie's proposal. EdVisions was formed and included all of the school's employees, as well as people who had worked on creating New Country. EdVisions would provide New Country's teachers under contract, and they—not an administration or a board—would make the educational decisions, control the budget, set salaries, and determine professional development. Thomas recalls telling her colleagues that "if we didn't make history with our unique school design, we were certainly going to with the teacher ownership and professionalism model" (Thomas, n.d., para. 10).

On its website, EdVisions (http://www.edvisions.com/) elaborates on its founding and mission:

> The cooperative is based upon educational entrepreneurship rather than district master agreements. It essentially replaces union arrangements by creating a professional association of teacher/owners that contract with a school board to supply a learning program. It is based upon true site-based management and dynamic and flexible decision making. The cooperative provides continuing growth for educators in a professional association of like-minded educators. . . .

> The Articles of Incorporation say that the cooperative is to: "provide employment and income to its members in a manner that would permit them, individually and in concert with one another, in a cooperative structure, to employ their skills, talents and resources for the development and implementation of quality instructional programs."

The website further notes that EdVisions is based on the premise "that teacher leadership is not about power, but about mobilizing the largely untapped attributes of teachers to strengthen student performance by working collaboratively in a shared capacity." And because "cooperatives are democratically owned and managed, they are a model for adolescents who must learn to live in, and participate in, a democratic society."

EdVisions recognizes that teaching is not an end in itself. The ultimate goal is to help youngsters grow and learn. To "stay in business," teacher partnerships must satisfy their clients. That means they must be at the leading edge of their profession and constantly look for effective and innovative ways to help students learn. Members are expected to develop and carry out their own professional development plan.

Although EdVisions first offered its professional services to Minnesota New Country School, it now has about 35 schools across the country and is a nationally recognized model for project-based learning. Several books have been written about the EdVisions model, including *Teachers as Owners*, edited by Edward J. Dirkswager (2002).

In a recent Education Evolving paper, Ted Kolderie (2010) has "kicked it up a notch" by suggesting that teacher unions take the lead in the school reform movement, essentially by following the EdVisions model. He suggests that unions propose that teachers will "take responsibility for student and school success . . . if teachers can control what matters for student and school success" (p. 14). Surveys have indicated that younger union members would choose this larger role if they had the opportunity. There is evidence that "where teachers do control their work, their (and their students') attitudes and behaviors change dramatically" (p. 14). For example, students say they enjoy school more and feel their teachers care more about them. Teachers with ideas about practice and learning enjoy the freedom to implement them. Having more say about the process of teaching and learning and more responsibility for the whole enterprise makes their work more fulfilling. They are more like partners with their students in the adventure of learning.

The Los Angeles board of education is about to test the hypothesis. The board turned over control of 30 schools to nonprofit educational organizations formed by teachers (Blume, 2010). Twelve of the schools are chronically poor schools, and 18 are new schools.

Everything would change if the school and its teachers were to be given real control over the learning in the school. As Kolderie writes, "If [authority and accountability] are not combined at the school, for heaven's sake, at what level *can* they be effectively combined?" (2010, p. 14).

| CHAPTER 17 |

A Matter of Choice

ASSUMPTION: *Choice is essential to a new-schools strategy. Students and their parents should be able to choose their school and other educational opportunities through open enrollment in states and districts and unlimited charter schools.*

Henry Ford said of his Model T: "Any customer can have a car painted any color that he wants so long as it is black."

Today, in our capitalist, consumerist society, we have a stupefying number of choices in virtually every aspect of life, from buying a pair of socks to buying a yacht to choosing a hospital or a real estate agent. But in public education, the majority of students can attend any public school they want so long as it's in their neighborhood.

Beginning in 1991, the situation began to change. Minnesota adopted the first statewide open-enrollment law. Other states followed suit, and within four years, "choice" became the new buzzword of the school reform movement.

In those early days, "choice" was a catchall term that included not only open enrollment and charter schools, but tuition tax credits and vouchers redeemable by private schools. Unfortunately, the hit-and-run nature of politics did not encourage policymakers to distinguish among the various forms of choice, so one was either for it or against it.

The 1988 Republican platform supported tax credits for private school tuition and mentioned choice several times, calling for "voucher systems or other means of encouraging competition among public schools." By 1989, 13 states had passed legislation giving parents the right to choose public schools outside their own districts. A dozen additional states were considering choice legislation, and many districts across the country were establishing public-school-choice plans. A year later, John E. Chubb and Terry M. Moe (1990) published their controversial *Politics, Markets, and America's Schools*, arguing that the key to successful education in the United States was to introduce "free market competition" into the monopoly of public education by awarding students a financial stipend that could be used in private schools.

Choice was a hot issue in the 1992 presidential campaign. President George H. W. Bush, who had not publicly supported private school vouchers, strongly endorsed them and included $200 million in his budget proposal to offer incentives to school districts to adopt voucher programs that would offset tuition at private schools.

Not surprisingly, teacher unions, liberals, and most elected Democrats were staunchly anti-choice. They argued that choice was designed to undermine public schools, especially since the GOP was pushing the concept of "privatization" to reduce the size of government and turn many of its functions over to the private sector. In a special report, *Education Week* said "choice" had become "the most politically loaded word on the social horizon" ("Matter of Choice," 1992, para. 2).

Shortly after the Chubb and Moe book was published, I moderated a discussion between Chubb and Bella Rosenberg of the American Federation of Teachers on the topic of choice. After a gentle and polite beginning, the dialogue turned to vouchers and quickly degenerated into a flurry of strident exchanges between the two. Increasingly anxious about being in the line of fire, I abruptly thanked everybody and ended the session a tad early.

Choice and Charter Schools

In recent years, the debate over choice has tended to focus mainly on charter schools. Vouchers and tuition tax credits remain controversial even though the District of Columbia, Cleveland, Milwaukee, and several other cities offer them and the U.S. Supreme Court ruled that Cleveland's voucher program is constitutional (Walsh,

2002). Today the voucher debate is more a matter of rhetorical jousting than serious political argument. According to the Friedman Foundation for Educational Choice (2009), 160,000 students in the United States currently are being served by one of 24 school choice programs, including voucher programs, in 15 states and the District of Columbia.

Although, as must be evident from several previous chapters, I strongly support chartering and both statewide and districtwide open enrollment, I do not endorse vouchers. In fact, when the National Research Council recommended a nationwide voucher program in a report on school financing several years ago, I was surprised and mystified. A voucher program here and there would generate more noise than real change in the overall public education system. But if we gave every student a chit to attend any public or private school, I believe we would create confusion and controversy and do nothing to improve education.

For a national voucher program to be justifiable, the demand would presumably exceed supply, and the result would likely be chaotic. Existing private schools do not have nearly the capacity to absorb significant numbers of transfer students. High-quality charter schools could not be established fast enough to accommodate more than a fraction of the students leaving their current schools. I can't even imagine the effect on teachers and how they would be distributed. Such a program would wreak havoc on the schools that lost students.

In calling for a new-schools strategy of education improvement, I recognize the necessity (and desirability) of steady year-by-year growth. The goal is to increase educational opportunities for a diverse student population and to create high-quality innovative schools as an alternative to the conventional school. But, their shortcomings notwithstanding, the nation's schools enroll some 54 million students. A sudden disruption like a national voucher program would hurt our children, our schools, and the larger society.

Competition: An Overstated Threat

The claim that free-market competition will improve the present school system is greatly overstated. Predictions that schools would have to change voluntarily to compete for students and money have been proven wrong. In fact, even when NCLB mandated that schools make annual improvement or face sanctions, thousands of schools did not change. Among NCLB sanctions is a provision that parents may choose a better school if their child's school does not improve.

A few years ago, the superintendent of the Providence School District wrote to the parents of students in a low-performing middle school telling them that No Child Left Behind compelled him to inform them of the school's persistent poor performance and let them know that they could transfer their child to a better school. However, he continued, he was sorry to inform them that there was no higher-performing middle school in the district. So much for public school choice.

Open enrollment, across state or district lines, and the growth in chartering do introduce an element of competition. Steady, incremental increases in alternative educational opportunities and the ability of parents and students to choose among them could well provide a compelling incentive for existing schools to look for more effective ways to serve their clientele.

If students choose alternative schools or approaches to education, the conventional school loses students and the state funds that follow them. Indeed, this is one of the most common arguments against charter schools—that they siphon off the better students and drain funds away from existing schools. As in any enterprise without a captive market, schools soon get the message that they can only prevent the loss of students (and money) by satisfying their "customers." They can either change or do their best to thwart the growth of competition. Most have chosen the latter course.

For competition to trigger real change in existing schools, mechanisms and infrastructure must be in place to promote innovation and the sharing of ideas. Unfortunately, such mechanisms are rare. Good ideas and better practices do not spread easily in education. In many districts, charter schools and magnet schools have proven to be quite successful, but that seems to have no positive effect on other schools in the district.

I remember when Tony Alvarado turned New York City's District 2 into one of the most successful public school jurisdictions in the city. Visitors from around the country came to see what the secret of success was. But few other districts in New York City were eager to learn and emulate. I have visited a dozen places that have attracted national attention for their successes but have failed to "scale up," as they say.

A decade or so ago, the superintendent of Memphis schools ordered that every school choose one of several reform models. Her plan ended in failure, largely because the culture of any given school will reject a different model that is imposed on it, much as a body rejects a foreign organ transplant.

The Rarity of Replication

There have been many attempts to replicate successful schools and successful practices, but few that have worked and endured. Rhode Island's governor appointed an urban education task force in early 2009, led by Warren Simmons of the Annenberg Institute at Brown. I cochaired the innovations subcommittee, and we recommended a "zone of innovation"—a nongeographical space where new schools, mostly chartered, could try new ideas without the traditional limitations. Knowing that some mechanism would be needed to inform and transmit successes to conventional schools and districts, we also recommended a new Center for Innovation, which would be a quasi-public, 501(c)(3) organization to sponsor and promote new ideas and procedures and enlist the cooperation of community-based organizations to help.

Because districts have a poor record in establishing innovative, unconventional schools (with some notable exceptions), charter schools are a central part of a new-schools strategy for improving student learning. They are public schools and receive public funds; they are exempt from some regulations but must meet state standards and comply with equity and safety provisions. Often they are not required to unionize.

Chartering laws have made it possible to create new public schools that are different from traditional schools and from each other. By providing different models of schooling, they begin to accommodate the diversity of today's student body and offer alternatives to the batch-process delivery of a one-size-fits-all education to all students. At their best, charter schools are creative and committed, succeeding with the most disadvantaged students.

Ray Budde, a professor at the University of Massachusetts, Amherst, first proposed that charter schools be established in the United States in a paper he presented in 1974 (Kolderie, 2005). He envisioned a legally and financially autonomous public school (without tuition, religious affiliation, or selective student admissions) that would operate much like a private business—free from many state laws and district regulations, and accountable more for student outcomes than for seat time and test scores.

Albert Shanker, president of the American Federation of Teachers, endorsed the idea in 1988, calling for "charter schools" and "schools of choice" as a way of improving public education. When he called for the reform of the public schools by establishing "charter schools" or "schools of choice," Shanker imagined that such schools would be created and run by teachers—an idea whose time has not yet really come (Kolderie, 2005).

Minnesota adopted the first charter school law, in 1991, followed by California a year later. By 2009, 40 states and the District of Columbia had enacted charter school laws (USCharterSchools.org, n.d.).

Conventions and Constraints

Unfortunately, not all charter schools are innovative and successful. Too many have been created to avoid teacher unions and in most respects resemble conventional schools. Several years ago, I attended a meeting of charter school authorizers in New York City. A couple of the most prominent speakers noted proudly that their charter schools were in compliance with NCLB. A charter school that is simply a conventional school with a different form of governance undermines the purpose of chartering.

Skeptics argue that charter schools are no better at educating kids than traditional schools are. Proponents claim the opposite. A 2009 study by the Center for Research on Education Outcomes at Stanford University concludes that there is a "wide variation in performance." The study reveals that 17 percent of charter schools provide superior education opportunities for their students, but nearly half of the charter schools nationwide have results that are no different from the local public school options, and more than one-third—37 percent—deliver learning results that are significantly worse than those that their students would have realized had they remained in traditional public schools.

But to stress what I've said earlier, this study and most others compare standardized test scores to judge student and school performance. Such scores are woefully inadequate and inappropriate to determine how successful nontraditional charter schools are.

The fact is that chartering is simply a form of governance that permits a school to be innovative but doesn't *require* it to be. Ultimately, the success of chartering will be determined by what occurs inside schools and not by their form of governance. Chartering does not automatically guarantee high-quality education, but it creates an environment in which educational entrepreneurs can pursue innovative policies and practices that may ultimately help fulfill our obligation to students and our promise to society.

State chartering laws leave considerable room for improvement. Such laws should require a charter applicant to spell out how the school it creates will differ from a conventional school; they should be more thoughtful about who can authorize a charter and under what conditions; charter schools should receive the same funding that other schools in the district receive; the law should provide space or funds to acquire space for charters; there should be no arbitrary cap on the number of charters granted or the number of students in the state or district who can be enrolled in charter schools.

I have neither the expertise nor the space in this book to explore the specific provisions that might make charter laws more rational and successful, but if states believe chartering is an effective way to improve education, then they should do everything possible to make it work. It is illogical to pass chartering laws and then adopt policies that stifle them.

Opposition to Charter Schools

Teacher unions have opposed the charter movement and often managed to defeat or water down legislation. Some legislators and governors have actively denounced charter schools or have taken steps to restrain their growth. School districts have also generally resisted charter schools, arguing that they lure students (along with their state funds) away from traditional district schools, making a difficult funding problem even worse. They reject the argument that their loss of students and money is balanced by the fact that they don't have to educate those students. They can't reduce the staff or make other budget cuts, they say, because the transferring students come from different schools and different grade levels. The district still has to offer the same educational programs, district officials say, only with less money.

But the claim that the district still has to offer the same educational programs is a main reason a second strategy is needed. If those who run the system insist on doing everything they have always done in the same way for the same or greater cost, then change and innovation will not come.

In 2010, recanting her firm convictions on school reform, Diane Ravitch denounced school choice in her book *The Death and Life of the Great American School System: How Testing and Choice Are Undermining Education*. She had been an early and ardent supporter of choice and vouchers and as a senior official in the U.S. Education Department worked to make her beliefs a reality.

Her arguments against choice have been used for decades by critics. She writes that charter schools will undermine (she says "destroy") public education, not saying what she must know is true: that charters *are* public schools. If they undermine anything, it will be poor-performing conventional schools.

Ravitch goes on to repeat the claim that charters are draining away scarce resources from "public schools." Obviously she meant to say from "*other* public schools." When students leave a district school to enroll in a charter, they take the state funding with them. That is the way it works when a student transfers from one public school to a school in a different district, like, for example, when students migrate from city schools to suburban schools.

Ravitch also claims charters admit students by lottery, leaving the district schools with those students who are the hardest to educate; because students who apply to a charter come from families that obviously care about education, charters attract better students. Hogwash. Being public schools, charters are obligated to accept any student who applies, and a lottery is used only when there are more applicants than seats—which is a fairer way than the admission requirement imposed by colleges and private schools. If the parents of students in charter schools care more about education, they shouldn't be punished. Aren't caring parents what we're always calling for?

Ravitch is well enough known and respected to fuel the dispute over charters. So policymakers should consider carefully the perplexing questions raised by her (and others') criticisms. Why are students leaving traditional schools to attend charter schools? Are the new schools offering something the district schools don't? Are the traditional schools so unattractive that students are eager to leave them? How do attendance and dropout rates compare? Should a school be held harmless when it loses students and funding to another school?

When a business loses market share, it must improve its product or its marketing practices to recapture lost income. If that doesn't work, a company must find ways to become more efficient and more effective to reduce costs. If that doesn't work, the next step is bankruptcy.

Why should schools be held harmless if students leave a district school for one that they believe better meets their needs? States don't hold urban schools harmless when their students migrate to the suburbs.

Critics of charter schools say they should be held accountable the way conventional schools are. In fact, they are more accountable because the charter is granted for a limited term (usually three to five years) and can be withdrawn if the schools do not fulfill their contractual obligations. If that were true for district schools, many more would have closed over the past few decades.

Charter schools are also required to meet the same standards and give the same statewide tests as district schools. A more fair and rational system would permit charter schools to develop their own equally high standards for approval by the chartering agency. And because their curricula and pedagogies may be so different as to be incompatible with statewide standardized tests, charter schools would be better judged on the basis of the multiple measures discussed in an earlier chapter: attendance, graduation rates, and participation in postsecondary programs.

The typical response to those suggestions is that charter schools should not be exempt from rules; we should have a level playing field, and all schools should play by the same rules. The problem is that the playing field and the rules are determined by the conventional schools, which don't work for a majority of the kids attending them. To demand that new, innovative schools be like most existing schools is to undermine the purpose and promise of charter schools and to perpetuate mediocrity.

One of the more outlandish criticisms of charter schools appeared in a recent report by the Civil Rights Project at UCLA (Frankenberg, Siegel-Hawley, & Wang, 2010). It declared that charter schools are more racially segregated than traditional public schools in practically every state and large urban area. The complaint is that too many charter schools lack diversity because a majority of their students are minority students. This prompted one congressional aide to say that the study finds that some charter schools "aren't white enough."

As noted earlier, being public schools, charter schools don't have selective admission requirements and use a lottery to choose students only if the school is oversubscribed. The question that should be asked is why a disproportionate number of minority and poor students are choosing to attend charter schools.

The most obvious victims of poor-performing schools are minority and immigrant students who qualify for federal free-meal programs. They are on the lower side of the achievement gap. They drop out of school at higher rates. They attend and complete college at lower rates. They are now generally isolated in urban and rural schools. It should be neither a surprise nor a cause for concern if they take advantage of choice to go to a school they believe is better for them.

Affluent families already have choice. The "tuition" they pay to attend suburban schools is the price of a house in that district. When these families decide to choose charter schools, we will know that the second strategy has become the main strategy.

CHAPTER 18

Schools for Digital Natives

ASSUMPTION: *If schools are to adequately serve students who have grown up in the digital age, they must incorporate and integrate the new technology into their structure, curriculum, pedagogy, and culture in ways that enhance learning.*

"It is amazing to me," writes educator and consultant Marc Prensky, "how in all the hoopla and debate these days about the decline of education in the U.S. we ignore the most fundamental of its causes. Our students have changed radically. Today's students are no longer the people our educational system was designed to teach" (2001, para. 1).

Prensky calls today's students "digital natives" and most of the rest of us who entered the world of technology later in life "digital immigrants." His message is clear: schools must move quickly into the digital age, or they will become increasingly irrelevant to their students and the larger society.

Instead of just waiting for schools to "move quickly" or whole-heartedly into the digital age, we should seize the opportunities offered by a new strategy of new schools to advance the concept of online learning. In the 2008–09 school year, 190 virtual charter schools were in operation nationwide (Moe & Chubb, 2009), and that number is expected to continue to grow. The schools are good examples of the "disruptive innovation" that Clay Christensen writes about (Christensen, Horn, & Johnson, 2008).

As I was working on this chapter, the Obama administration announced its first national educational technology plan,

"Transforming American Education: Learning Powered by Technology" (Office of Educational Technology, 2010). Remarkably in synch with a new-schools strategy, the plan stresses the importance of using technology to customize learning for each student.

In commenting on the plan, Karen Cator, the director of the Office of Educational Technology for the U.S. Department of Education, said, "Learning is at the center of the whole plan. Technology allows us to create more engaging and compelling learning opportunities for students and allows us to *personalize the learning experience*" (Ash, 2010, para. 6, emphasis added).

The plan urges educators and policymakers to challenge the basic assumptions of conventional K–12 education, including the sacred cows of seat time, the ubiquitous Carnegie unit, and the grouping of students by age. Ms. Cator also says curriculum, assessment, and teacher education will need to change to enrich student experiences. The plan recognizes the growing importance of online learning, citing it as a way to "extend the learning day, week, or year."

Technology Gets a Toehold

Clearly, progress has been made since President Bill Clinton urged that all students have access to computers that are connected to the Internet and each other and run software programs that are linked to the curriculum and schools.

Education Week Digital Directions, in its reporting on a Sloan Consortium study that used survey data collected in 2007–08, says "the number of K–12 students using online courses has increased dramatically in the past few years" (Davis, 2009, para. 1). The report cites researchers' estimates "that more than a million public school students now take classes online, a 47 percent increase from the consortium's original K–12 survey done in the 2005–06 school year" (para. 2). According to the report, more than 650 school districts across the country "are offering online-only courses or courses that mix online and traditional instruction, and 75 percent of those districts had one or more students enrolled in a fully online course" (para. 3).

According to Susan Patrick (personal communication, August 2010), CEO of the International Association for K–12 Online Learning (iNACOL), there are 46 states with policies, programs, or initiatives in K–12 online learning, and the number of student enrollments in K–12 online courses was an estimated 1.5 million in 2009.

The terms "cyber school" and "virtual school" and their synonyms can be confusing. A paper by the Education Commission of the States (Long, 2004) says the terms "are applied to a myriad of K–12 learning activities and programs." They include cyber schools operated by public school districts and other local education agencies; cyber schools operated by state education agencies; cyber schools operated by colleges and universities; cyber charter schools; and cyber schools operated by regional agencies and consortiums of educational entities, nonprofit organizations, and for-profit organizations. Other categories of cyber schools exist too, including private and for-profit schools.

Those are encouraging gains, largely because they increase flexibility in scheduling, offer courses not available in all traditional schools, and allow students who fall behind to make up credits. They allow "digital natives" to work at home in a more comfortable and familiar milieu.

But more often than not, virtual schools and cyber schools are essentially traditional schools on the Internet. Twenty-five states had virtual schools in 2008, enrolling about 317,000 students (Patrick, 2010). Created by state law or by a state agency, the virtual school is not intended to replace the traditional school, but rather to supplement it by offering online courses, without really changing the school's core function.

The Florida Virtual School exemplifies the "supplementary" nature of online programs. It is the nation's largest Internet public school, enrolling more than 70,000 students in 2008–09, some from abroad (Florida Virtual School, n.d.). The statewide school, financed by the state, offers more than 100 credit courses that duplicate and sometimes augment the conventional school curriculum. Florida Virtual helps its students attain the course credits required for a diploma. The school has over 1,200 staff members, and all of its teachers are certified, including 100 who are National Board certified.

Individual cyber schools are different from state virtual schools. They are full-fledged, full-time online schools, exemplified by the Ohio Virtual Academy, the Pennsylvania Virtual Charter School, and the Wisconsin Virtual Academy. These schools receive state funding and provide a complete free public school education, generally to elementary and middle school students.

While cyber schools may differ somewhat from each other, they are structured much like a traditional school. The Pennsylvania Virtual Charter School, for example, says on its website (pavcsk12.org) that it offers "a structured yet flexible, interactive environment to prepare students for optimal academic and social development from Kindergarten through 12th grade." Its mission is "to provide Pennsylvania students with an excellent education, grounded in high academic standards, which will help them achieve their full scholastic and social potential," and it envisions reaching its goals for students, teachers, and parents "through the effective use of technology."

The Need for Bolder Action

Cyber schools are poking at the traditional structure and culture of the conventional school, but even they do not take advantage of the full benefits of the new technology. The Pennsylvania school's website, for instance, lists the following as reasons why parents and students should choose the school: a K–12 curriculum "based on traditional core subject matter"; academic accountability; and engagement of all students in "reading, writing, calculating, speaking, listening, acting, drawing, painting, and more."

The number of cyber charter schools has been rising. In their latest book, *Liberating Learning: Technology, Politics, and the Future of American Education* (2009), Terry M. Moe and John E. Chubb compiled data showing that as of 2009, there were 190 virtual charter schools across the nation, enrolling 190,000 students, with Ohio and Pennsylvania leading the way.

The growth in virtual schools and online programs in the existing system is encouraging because it validates the use of the new technology and suggests its great potential in education. But there is little evidence as yet to suggest that the technology is enhancing student learning to a significant degree or freeing students from the archaic structure and operation of the conventional school. In fact, critics believe that the new technology is being hemmed in by the ironclad borders of curriculum, time, and traditional instruction. In *Disrupting Class*, Clay Christensen writes the following:

> Classrooms look largely the same as they did before the personal computer revolution, and the teaching and learning processes are similar to what they were in the days before computers.... The billions schools have spent on computers have had little effect—save possibly to increase costs and draw resources away from other school priorities. They haven't brought schools any closer to a child-centric classroom. (Christensen, Horn, & Johnson, 2008, p. 72)

Rethinking Education in the Age of Technology: The Digital Revolution and Schooling in America, by Allan Collins and Richard Halverson (2009), makes the same point, arguing that education cannot be fixed by fixing the schools, which they call a 19th century invention trying to cope in the 21st century. If schools cannot change fast enough to keep pace with the advances in learning technologies, learning will leave schooling behind.

Several studies report that teachers, in general, are not taking advantage of the new technology, and students are being asked to "power down" their electronic devices at school. For example, most of the high school students surveyed by Project Tomorrow, a nonprofit organization based in Irvine, California, "do not believe that they are being well prepared for the technology demands of the marketplace" (Manzo, 2009, "Students Suggest Changes," para. 1). Many middle and high school respondents said that they are unable to use technology effectively in school because of restrictions on computer time, blocked access to websites, and a ban on mobile devices in school. More than 280,000 K–12 students across the country took part in the 2008 online poll, along with 28,000 teachers, 21,000 parents, and 3,000 administrators.

The Imperative of School Change

If technology is not being used to its full potential in schools, one main reason is that it is incompatible with the way schools are organized and operated. Jamming new technology into a curriculum and a pedagogy that are essentially obsolete and ineffective with most of today's students is a waste of time and money.

The Obama administration's educational technology plan is correct when it points out that curriculum, assessment, and teacher education will need to change if the full power of technology is to be used to enrich student experiences.

Squeezing technology into the conventional curriculum and schedule is like using a high-powered sports car to deliver the mail. One of the advantages of the Internet is that it is nonlinear; it allows a student to follow a path in which one learning experience can lead to another. A student doing an essay on the Castro reign in Cuba may wander off to read about José Martí and his poems and essays, Cuba's break from Spain, the tradition of dictatorships in Latin America, and the long and turbulent relationship between the United States and Cuba.

I can almost hear the teacher saying, "focus, concentrate on your essay topic." But an essay should not be an end in itself; if the purpose of schooling is to open young minds and stimulate curiosity, the student's journey through history is a laudable accomplishment. Personalization is about much more than giving a student a computer and allowing him to work at home on his own schedule. It is, as I have said before, giving students a voice in deciding what they want to know and do.

Still, the question of whether online education is significantly improving student learning is yet to be answered. The movement is so new that only a few solid research studies have made the case for online learning at the K–12 level.

A meta-analysis of online learning studies conducted by SRI International for the U.S. Department of Education concluded that "on average, students in online learning conditions performed better than those receiving face-to-face instruction" (Lohr, 2009, para. 1). Most of the studies analyzed, however, dealt with older learners. Nonetheless, the half dozen or so focusing on precollegiate students were positive.

Even if research becomes available comparing online student learning with conventional school learning, it should be suspect because it is likely to be based on test scores. One of the primary arguments for online learning is that it personalizes education to a greater degree and recognizes that children learn in different ways and at different speeds whether in a classroom or online. To average out test scores to compare one mode of instruction with another is unreliable and perhaps misleading. Bubble-in test scores are no more valid as a measure of learning in online learning situations than in conventional schools. What matters is how the technology is used and for what purposes.

I submit that the new technology is being used more effectively in new schools that commit to personalized education and individual learning plans than in virtual schools or cyber schools. In online programs in conventional schools, virtual schools, or cyber schools, students are still functioning in the standards-based accountability model, still being told what they must know and when they must know it. The advantages of online learning for them are real but limited.

Students in new schools that allow students to develop their own individual learning plans and pursue their interests are empowered by the new technology. For them, the Internet is a portal to a world of ideas and knowledge that they can explore in ways never before possible. The Internet puts a library at their fingertips; it permits them to transport themselves to different lands and different times almost instantly. They can learn through simulations, engage the world's great minds, view magnificent works of art, hear music, see videos, and communicate instantly with others almost anywhere in the world. And they can do all of this in a nourishing environment with the help and guidance of a caring advisor.

Technology also has the potential to enhance learning by revolutionizing educational testing. It can make conventional paper-and-pencil tests obsolete. A study by the Center for the Study of Testing, Evaluation, and Educational Policy (CSTEEP) at Boston College confirms that written tests administered via paper and pencil may significantly underestimate the capabilities of computer-savvy students (Delaney, 1999). The results showed that students accustomed to writing on a computer did substantially better when they composed test answers on the computer instead of in hand-writing. The results paralleled those of an earlier CSTEEP study, "in which the effects were so large that when tech-savvy students wrote on paper, only 30 percent performed at a 'passing' level, but when they wrote on computers (without access to word processing tools such as spell check or grammar check), 67 percent 'passed'" (Delaney, 1999, para. 4). The test questions were from the highly regarded Massachusetts Comprehensive Assessment System and the National Assessment of Educational Progress.

Computers and electronic technology offer far more benefits than simply providing a keyboard instead of a pencil and paper. Computer-assisted testing can include dynamic visuals, use interactivity, and report scores immediately. It makes possible quality formative assessment that closely links questions to the material studied.

A good fit with personalized education, computer-based assessments can be tailored to test each student differently based on individual knowledge level. In response to a student's answers, the computer program can adjust the difficulty of the questions upward or downward. And it can simultaneously record the student's responses, progress on the test, and score. The assessments let teachers see the students as individuals and provide them with detailed information on a student's progress in learning. Not incidentally, students tend to find such tests more stimulating than linear paper tests.

Not counting any necessary investment in equipment and software, computer-assisted assessments are more efficient and cheaper than the traditional paper-and-pencil tests. They can be used either as formative assessments or tests for accountability.

Challenges of Technology

The rise of technology presents challenges to the institutions that prepare K–12 teachers. As with schools, the new technology should be integrated into the curricula and pedagogy of college and university teacher preparation programs. Clearly, the new technology will be accepted and used in schools only to the extent that teachers understand it, know how to use it, and see its potential for helping students to learn. Even though aspiring teachers are probably more computer-savvy, teacher preparation programs should emphasize the uses, benefits, and limitations of the new technology.

The potential benefits of technology in helping students learn are so obvious that one might assume it would be welcomed enthusiastically. The assumption would be wrong. Despite the rapid growth in online programs, they face opposition from some policymakers and teacher unions. Money is the key issue. Just as they charge that charter schools drain students and funding away from conventional schools, critics argue that online programs are diverting much-needed resources from conventional schools.

Another topic of debate is whether students can learn effectively without face-to-face engagement with their teachers and peers. And some fear that students working at home without the constant supervision they get in conventional classrooms will procrastinate or waste time or cheat—all vices routinely committed in conventional schools.

That fear leads some lawmakers to drag their feet on approving state per-pupil funding for kids who work at home. Some also feel it is an inappropriate use of public money to fund students who aren't physically in a school. Can a virtual school be a real school? Moreover, isn't this mainly a subsidy for students who are home-schooled?

Others see large sums of money flowing to online programs and charters that are not as carefully regulated as districts. They are nervous because virtual charter schools often partner with for-profit corporations, like K–12 Inc., which works with schools in 17 states. Cases of funds being misused in virtual charter schools and school officials behaving improperly have also generated opposition. Again, the misuse of funds and improper behavior by officials is not exactly unheard of in regular district schools.

Online learning is a good example of Clayton Christensen's "disruptive innovation" that can lead to changes in the educational world. And it is growing rapidly and becoming more widely accepted. Still, there is a long way to go to maximize and extend the benefits of technology to the 54 million students who currently attend about 100,000 schools in some 14,500 districts.

A new-schools strategy can help accomplish that goal by showing the potential of technology as a powerful tool for personalization, learning, and assessment.

Can We Get There from Here?

Perhaps the most discouraging lesson I've learned in more than 30 years studying K–12 education is that the vast majority of the public, parents, and opinion leaders accept most of the existing system as a given. They do so because they assume that is the way the schools are supposed to be. They cannot imagine schools that are much different from the ones they attended. And even those who are dissatisfied with the status quo rarely have the information, the expertise, or the power to change it. Finally, the resistance to significant change is so entrenched in several power centers that it is intimidating and risky to challenge the major assumptions on which our education system is based.

This was driven home to me as I was writing the final chapters of this book. On our "annual retreat," two former colleagues and I were sharing a converted barn on a hilltop in Big Sur, California. With the golden hills around us and the Pacific Ocean stretching endlessly ahead of us, this was clearly not the time or place to be discussing education. But at times the conversation slipped into the topic and into vigorous argument.

Both men have teenagers who attend "good" suburban schools. One of my friends had served for several years as chairman of his local school board and remains as a member. Both had spent at least two decades working on education publications.

In one discussion, I made several of the main arguments of this book, laying out in brief the case for an alternative strategy for educational improvement based on the creation of new schools. I was surprised by their passionate resistance to my case. They acknowledged that public schools are not performing as well as we wish they would, but they insisted that most of the pathology is in urban schools and was mainly the result of attitudes and behavior of students and their parents. Although they acknowledged that these attitudes and the resulting behavior are in large measure due to socioeconomic factors, they insisted that students and parents are not meeting their responsibilities for ensuring that kids receive a good education. Most of the schools in suburbs and smaller communities, they said, were doing OK.

My friends were not enthusiastic about charter schools, fearing that they were not academically rigorous enough and had lower expectations for their students. This, they believe, is a return to the tracking of past years. And, of course, charters take resources from district schools.

They asserted the need for common standards, a common curriculum, and standardized testing to ensure that every student has the opportunity to acquire the knowledge and skills needed to get a good and productive job. To have lower standards or less demanding academic programs for minority, immigrant, and poor children would consign them and future generations to less productive lives and would hurt the society as well.

To my suggestion that young people, especially high school students, be permitted to help shape their own curriculum and follow their own interests, my friends replied that too many adolescents lack the judgment and experience to make choices like that. They need to be directed to do what will be in their best interest. Personalizing education for all students was not practical, they argued, and I underestimate the challenges of running a school and meeting the myriad demands they face.

Of course, I had heard these arguments many times before, but here were two well-informed, well-educated, broad-minded friends looking at the same issues I was struggling with and coming out on the opposite side.

This was a perplexing experience for me, and I have pondered that exchange in the days since. I recognize, of course, that their arguments have some truth in them. Indeed, I am grateful to them for their articulate disagreement because they gave me the conclusion of this book by confirming what I already knew instinctively—namely, that our present system of public education cannot be transformed. It is too complex, too political, and too personal for major systemic change to occur.

Power Centers That Stifle Change

A number of different power centers, each with its own agenda and special interests, make it impossible to change public education in any substantial way. Although these power centers rarely are able by themselves to make important and enduring changes to improve education, one or two of them can veto or derail such efforts. Consider the following nine formidable power centers:

- **The State**. Public education is a government institution. The states' constitutions give them the ultimate responsibility for and authority over the system. State policymakers must approve the adoption and funding of any significant departure from the status quo. Legislatures and state departments of education enact laws and regulations that define the context in which education is delivered in the state.
- **School Boards**. The states delegate to locally elected or appointed school boards the daily control and oversight of the public schools. School boards hire the superintendents and approve hiring of administrators and teachers. They negotiate contracts with the unions and approve the district budget. In some cities, mayors and city councils have more influence on schools than school boards.
- **Superintendents.** The superintendent is the CEO of the district, charged with its daily management (including curriculum and scheduling), development of plans and objectives, hiring of principals, supervision of personnel, formulation of the budget, relations with the community, and more.
- **The Principal**. The principal is the chief operating officer of the individual school with duties similar to those of the superintendent but at a building level. Commensurate with district policies and the union contract, principals usually have some responsibility for choosing teachers and

overseeing them. They submit budgets to the superintendent and are responsible for the disbursement of the funds
allocated. In the best cases, they are also the "principal
teacher."

- **Teachers.** As individuals, their power is pretty much limited
to the classroom and their students. Collectively they wield
significant power in the operations of the schools and the
district. The teacher unions have negotiated contracts over
the years that influence scheduling and work hours, salaries
and benefits, personnel evaluation, hiring and firing. Their
members often serve in the legislature or are related to
legislators.

- **Parents.** For the most part, they limit their involvement in
education to PTA and PTO activities and making sure their
children conform to school policies related to such matters as attendance and homework. Although they seldom
act collectively or assertively, parents can exert significant influence on schools and districts when they become
unhappy with some policy or procedure that affects them or
their children. The decision to close a school is a common
example of a situation that leads parents to rise in protest.
Generally, however, they are passive and their power is
dormant.

- **The Public.** People in general are apathetic about schools
and education. In opinion polls, they acknowledge the
importance of education and profess to support it, though
they may grumble and complain when test scores of individual schools are published in the local newspaper. The
public almost never asserts its ultimate control over the
system. Indeed, the percentage of voters who participate in
school board elections rarely rises above 20 percent. I would
be surprised if that many even know the name of their superintendent or school board chairman. Far fewer have any idea
what happens inside the school other than their recollection
of their own school days.

- **The Federal Government.** The feds have a disproportionate
influence in public education. Only about 7 percent of the
education dollar comes from the federal government (U.S.

Department of Education, n.d.). Although the U.S. Constitution mentions no federal responsibility for education, a host of laws over the decades have wrought major changes in schools. The U.S. Supreme Court has handed down decisions on the equality of education, the obligation of schools to special-needs students, the rights of students, and other important issues. Congress has enacted laws and provided funds that shape the ways schools deal with immigrant children, students from low-income families, and "gifted" students. No Child Left Behind was adopted to close the achievement gap, but it is so broad that there is almost no aspect of education that is not affected.

- **Lobbyists**. Education also has its share of lobbyists—though nothing comparable to the number in health care or energy policy. Most of the major education associations aren't located in Washington, D.C., because of the weather. They monitor federal and state education policy closely and speak out when their members' interest are somehow affected. Commercial enterprises use as much leverage as they can muster in the allocation of contracts for goods and services or influencing policies that they believe will harm their interests.

(Note that students are not considered a power center and have little say in their own education either individually or collectively.)

One would like to believe that all of these power centers have as their highest-priority goal to improve education for every student. In fact, our public education system is controlled by adults largely for the benefit of adults. Their actions invariably reflect their own economic and political interests. Even when there is consensus that some problem must be fixed, the resulting solution is almost always so compromised to accommodate all the vested interests that it doesn't work.

Rhetoric Versus Reality

Although the rhetoric of change is widely applauded, the reality is often bitterly divisive. In his campaign, Barack Obama promised dramatic change in health care, foreign policy, energy, education, and the economy. The public reaction was so overwhelmingly positive that he beat all the odds and became our first African American president. Every step he has taken to keep those promises since then has triggered furious opposition and lowered his public-approval rating.

Except for organized religion, no social institution has changed less in the past century than public education. Agriculture, transportation, medicine, communications, the military—all bear little resemblance to what they were a hundred years ago. Education looks the same today as it did then, except for the diversity of the students.

A superintendent of an Iowa school district once said to me, "We have a fine district. We always have had, and it hasn't changed a bit." He paused, then added, "except for the students." As the kids say: "Duh!"

The United States could grow and prosper a century ago when people were able to end their formal education by the 8th grade and still earn a good living, become part of a growing middle class, and make a positive contribution to their society. That's no longer the case. The issues we face are much more complicated and the stakes are higher. As the world changes more rapidly, the need for citizens—not just leaders—who are creative and imaginative, who can think clearly and act boldly becomes ever greater.

It is no exaggeration to say that our form of government is in some peril. A democratic government by definition depends on a well-informed citizenry—perhaps now more than ever. How can we serve as an example to the world of individual liberties if we compromise our values? How do we preserve human rights and civil liberties if we are ignorant of the Bill of Rights and the U.S. Constitution? How can we have a government "by the people," if too many people do not have informed opinions or are too apathetic to express them?

Gambling the Future

Deborah Meier, famous for her work in the Central Park East schools in Harlem, has said, "Thousands of years of history suggest that the schoolhouse as we know it is an absurd way to rear our young; it's contrary to everything we know about what it is to be a human being" (Littky & Grabelle, 1994, p. vii). And yet we continue as we always have, trying to make the schools of the past meet the awesome demands of the future.

History is replete with examples of the dire consequences of failing to change in the face of almost certain obsolescence. Clayton Christensen argues that the leading companies of the world have within themselves the seeds of failure (Christensen, Horn, & Johnson, 2008). If in the face of disrupting innovations they are unwilling or unable to change the way they operate, they are destined to fail.

That's certainly true of education. All, it seems, want better schools; they just don't want to change the ones they have.

Consequently, we continue to gamble our future on a system that is obviously not accomplishing our goals. We continue to bet everything on a single strategy that isn't working for a majority of our students—especially those who will soon be the majority in this nation.

So common sense suggests that, at the very least, we pursue a second strategy based on the very different set of assumptions outlined in the second part of this book. We need to adopt a parallel strategy of creating new schools of human scale that are innovative and very different from conventional schools and each other, that personalize education and evaluate learning based on student work and performance, not standardized test scores.

I am not suggesting that we give up on existing schools. We owe it to them and to the larger society to intensify our efforts to improve the conventional school. The existing system will be the primary institution for educating most of our children for many years to come.

Then why is a grassroots strategy to try something different perceived by so many as a threat? Surely an enterprise as massive as public education, protected and supported as it is by the nation's most powerful leaders, has nothing to fear from a fledgling effort to create new schools.

Perhaps one reason that education leaders and policymakers are worried about a second strategy to improve education is that they are not sure that standards-based accountability will get us where we need to be, and increasingly frustrated parents and students will leave conventional schools and turn to these innovative new schools.

In that case, we would be irresponsible not to embark on a separate, parallel strategy.

| REFERENCES |

Aarons, D. I. (2010a, March 2). More funding for principal training deemed vital. *Education Week*, *29*(23), 1, 14. Retrieved from http://www.edweek.org/ew/articles/2010/03/03/23capacity_ep.h29.html

Aarons, D. I. (2010b, March 15). Effect of Chicago's tougher science policy mixed. *Education Week*, *29*(27), 11. Retrieved from http://www.edweek.org/ew/articles/2010/03/15/27science.h29.html

ACT. (2010). *The condition of career and college readiness*. Retrieved September 14, 2010, from www.act.org/research/policymakers/cccr10/pdf/ConditionofCollegeandCareerReadiness2010.pdf

Adams, J. (2008, October 5). High-school heroes: When emergencies erupt, a squad of teen responders is ready. Science World. Retrieved from http://www.thefreelibrary.com/High-school+heroes%3A+when+emergencies+erupt,+a+squad+of+teen...-a0186433834

Advancement Project. (2010, March). *Test, punish and push out: How "zero tolerance" and high-stakes testing funnel youth into the school-to-prison pipeline*. Retrieved from http://www.advancementproject.org/sites/default/files/publications/rev_fin.pdf

After-School Corporation. (2008, June). *More time for learning: ELT initiatives and enrichment opportunities*. The Collaborative for Building After-School Systems.

Allen, J., & Allen, C. (2010, March 3). Escaping the high school twilight zone. *Education Week*, *29*(23), 22–23. Retrieved from http://www.edweek.org/ew/articles/2010/03/03/23allen_ep.h29.html

Alliance for Excellent Education. (2009, August). *The high cost of high school dropouts: What the nation pays for inadequate high schools* [Issue brief]. Retrieved from http://www.all4ed.org/files/HighCost.pdf

Alliance for Excellent Education. (2010, January). *The economic benefits from halving the dropout rate: A boom to businesses in the nation's largest metropolitan areas*. Retrieved from http://www.all4ed.org/files/NationalMSA.pdf

Archer, J. (2004, January 7). Foundation to expand state project on school leadership. *Education Week*, *23*(16), 14. Retrieved from http://www.edweek.org/ew/articles/2004/01/07/16wallace.h23.html

Ash, K. (2009, January 30). Hands-on learning vs. lecturing. *Education Week* Digital Education blog. Retrieved from http://blogs.edweek.org/edweek/DigitalEducation/2009/01/engaging_students_in_stem.html

Ash, K. (2010, March 5). U.S. Ed-Tech Plan prods K–12 to innovate; 1-to-1 computing seen as key shift. *Education Week*, *29*(24) 1, 16–17. Retrieved from http://www.edweek.org/ew/articles/2010/03/05/24edtech.h29.html

Ayers, W. (1993). *To teach: The journey of a teacher*. New York: Teachers College Press.

Balfanz, R., & Legters, N. (2004, September). *Locating the dropout crisis*. Johns Hopkins University. Retrieved from http://web.jhu.edu/CSOS/graduation-gap/power.html

Barton, P., & Coley, R. (2009, April). *Parsing the achievement gap II*. Educational Testing Service. Retrieved from http://www.ets.org/Media/Research/pdf/PICPARSINGII.pdf

Blume, H. (2010, January 27). L.A. groups bid to run 30 schools. *Los Angeles Times*. Retrieved from http://articles.latimes.com/2010/jan/27/local/la-me-lausd27-2010jan27

Borg, L. (2009, January 22). Survey gives voice to students' concerns about Providence schools. *The Providence Journal*. Retrieved from http://www.projo.com/ri/providence/content/young_voices_report_01-22-09_M7D1RB9_v22.3d552b5.html

Borg, L. (2010, April 13). Students, parents petition Providence RI School Board to continue Hope High School's innovations. *The Providence Journal*.

Bowles, A., & Brand, B. (2009). *Learning around the clock: Benefits of expanded learning opportunities for older youth*. Washington, DC: American Youth Policy Forum. Retrieved from http://www.aypf.org/documents/AYPF_ELOs_w-cvr.pdf

Bradley, A. (1995, February 1). Holmes Group urges overhaul of ed. schools. *Education Week*. Retrieved from http://www.edweek.org/ew/articles/1995/02/01/19holm.h14.html

Brady, M. (2006, August 29). Why thinking "outside the box" is not so easy (and why present reform efforts will fail). *Education Week*, *26*(1), 47–49. Retrieved from http://www.edweek.org/ew/articles/2006/08/30/01brady.h26.html

Brady, M. (2009, January 23). No dog left behind: The fallacy of "tough love" reform. *Education Week*, *28*(19), 24–25. Retrieved from http://www.edweek.org/ew/articles/2009/01/28/19brady.h28.html

Breslau, J. (2010, March 17). *The connection between health and high school dropout*. California Dropout Research Project. Retrieved from http://cdrp.ucsb.edu/dropouts/pubs_reports.htm

Bridgeland, J. M., Dilulio, J. J. Jr., & Burke Morison, K. (2006, March). *The silent epidemic: Perspectives of high school dropouts*. Civic Enterprises in association with Peter D. Hart Research Associates for the Bill & Melinda

Gates Foundation. Retrieved from http://www.civicenterprises.net/pdfs/thesilentepidemic3-06.pdf

Brill, S. (2009, August 31). The rubber room. *The New Yorker*. Retrieved from http://www.newyorker.com/reporting/2009/08/31/090831fa_fact_brill?printable=true

Carey, B. (2009, December 20). Studying young minds, and how to teach them. *The New York Times*. Retrieved from http://www.nytimes.com/2009/12/21/health/research/21brain.html

Cavanagh, S. (2007, June 12). What kind of math matters? *Education Week*, *26*(40), 21–23. Retrieved from http://www.edweek.org/ew/articles/2007/06/12/40math.h26.html

Cavanagh, S. (2008, September 24). Low performers found unready to take algebra. *Education Week*.

Center for Education Reform. (2009a). Charter Connection—All About Charter Schools. Retrieved from http://www.edreform.com/Issues/Charter_Connection/?All_About_Charter_Schools

Center for Education Reform. (2009b). K–12 facts. Retrieved from http://www.edreform.com/Fast_Facts/K12_Facts/

Center for Research on Education Outcomes (CREDO). (2009, June). Multiple choice: Charter schools in 16 states. Stanford, CA: Author.

Christensen, C. M. (2003). *The innovator's dilemma: The revolutionary book that will change the way you do business*. New York: Harper Business Essentials.

Christensen, C., Horn, M., & Johnson, C. (2008). *Disrupting class: How disruptive innovation will change the way the world learns*. New York: McGraw-Hill.

Chubb, J. E., & Moe, T. M. (1990). *Politics, markets, and America's schools*. Washington, DC: Brookings Institution.

Coleman, J. S. (Ed.). (1974). *Youth: Transition to adulthood*. Chicago: University of Chicago Press.

Collaborative for Building After-School Systems (CBASS). (2008). *More time for learning: ELT initiatives and enrichment opportunities*. Retrieved from http://www.afterschoolsystems.org/files/2124_file_ELT_BRIEF_2008.pdf

Collins, A., & Halverson, R. (2009). *Rethinking education in the age of technology: The digital revolution and schooling in America*. New York: Teachers College Press.

Conference Board, Partnership for 21st Century Skills, Corporate Voices for Working Families, and Society for Human Resource Management. (2006). *Are they really ready to work? Employers' perspectives on the basic knowledge and applied skills of new entrants to the 21st century U.S. workforce*. Retrieved from http://www.p21.org/documents/FINAL_REPORT_PDF09-29-06.pdf

Consortium for Policy Research in Education. (1995, June). *Helping teachers teach well: Transforming professional development*. CPRE policy brief.

Covey, S. R. (2004). *The seven habits of highly effective people*. New York: Free Press.

Cremin, L. A. (1976). *Public education*. New York: Basic Books.

Csikszentmihalyi, M. (1990). *Flow: The psychology of optimal experience*. New York: Harper & Row.

Daly, T., Keeling, D., Grainger, R., & Grundies, A. (2008). *Mutual benefits: New York City's shift to mutual consent in teacher hiring.* New Teacher Project.

Darling-Hammond, L., Haselkorn, D., & Bouw, J. (2009, April 1). Reforming teaching: Are we missing the boat? *Education Week, 28*(27), 30, 36. Retrieved from http://www.cateachercorps.org/downloads/reforming_teaching-education_week_april_1_2009.pdf

Data360. (2007). *High school graduation rates in select OECD countries.* Retrieved from http://www.data360.org/dsg.aspx?Data_Set_Group_Id=1653

Davenport, C., & Brown, E. (2009, November 5). Girding for an uphill battle for recruits. *Washington Post.* Retrieved from http://www.washingtonpost.com/wp-dyn/content/article/2009/11/04/AR2009110402899.html

Davis, M. R. (2009, January 26). Online course-taking shows dramatic growth. *Education Week, Digital Directions.* Retrieved from http://www.edweek.org/dd/articles/2009/01/26/04onlinestudy.h02.html

Delaney, P. (1999, July 22). Tests shortchange high-tech students. *The Boston College Chronicle, 7*(19). Retrieved from http://www.bc.edu/bc_org/rvp/pubaf/chronicle/v7/jl22/csteep.html

Department for Children, Schools, and Families. (2007, December). *The Children's Plan: Building brighter futures.* Retrieved from http://www.dcsf.gov.uk/childrensplan/downloads/The_Childrens_Plan.pdf

Dewey, J. (1916). *Democracy and education: An introduction to the philosophy of education.* New York: Macmillan.

Dillon, S. (2010, March 13). Obama calls for major change in education law. *The New York Times.* Retrieved from http://www.nytimes.com/2010/03/14/education/14child.html?pagewanted=print

DiMartino, J. (2007, April 23). Accountability, or mastery? *Education Week, 26*(34), 36, 44. Retrieved from http://www.edweek.org/ew/articles/2007/04/25/34dimartino.h26.html

Dirkswager, E. J. (Ed.). (2002). *Teachers as owners: A key to revitalizing public education.* Lanham, MD: Scarecrow Press.

Dubner, S. (2007, December 20). What should be done about standardized tests? A Freakonomics quorum. *The New York Times.* Retrieved from http://freakonomics.blogs.nytimes.com/2007/12/20/what-should-be-done-about-standardized-tests-a-freakonomics-quorum/.

Education Commission of the States (ECS). (n.d.). *High school graduation requirements: Mathematics.* Retrieved from http://mb2.ecs.org/reports/Report.aspx?id=900

Education Week. (1988, February 10). On the influence of the Army alpha "intelligence test." Retrieved from http://www.edweek.org/ew/articles/1988/02/10/07440022.h07.html

Education Week. (2007, June 12). Diplomas count: Ready for what? Preparing for college, careers, and life after high school. Retrieved from http://www.edweek.org/ew/toc/2007/06/12/index.html

Educational Networks. (n.d.). *Middle & high school websites.* Retrieved from http://www.educationalnetworks.net/ourwork/middleandhighschool.jsp

Educational Publishing. (2009, November 25). Graduation for All Act includes provisions aimed at instructional materials. Retrieved from http://edpublishing.wordpress.com/2009/11/25/graduation-for-all-act-includes-provisions-aimed-at-instructional-materials/

FairTest: The National Center for Fair and Open Testing. (2009, November). Teachers say too much testing undermines educational quality. Retrieved from http://www.fairtest.org/teachers-say-too-much-testing-undermines-education

Farkas, S., Johnson, J., & Duffett, A. (with Moye, L., & Vine, J.). (2003). *Stand by me: What teachers really think about unions, merit pay, and other professional matters*. Public Agenda. Retrieved from http://www.publicagenda.org/files/pdf/stand_by_me.pdf

Fields, G. (2008, October 21). The high school dropout's economic ripple effect. *The Wall Street Journal*. Retrieved from http://online.wsj.com/article/NA_WSJ_PUB:SB122455013168452477.html

Finn, C. E., Jr. (2002, May). Bureaucracy and school leadership—Policy research organization Public Agenda survey on finding strong leaders for schools. *Reason*. Retrieved from http://findarticles.com/p/articles/mi_m1568/is_1_34/ai_84841777/

Flexner, A. (1908). *The American college: A criticism*. New York: Century Co.

Florida Virtual School. (n.d.). Quick facts. Retrieved from http://www.flvs.net/areas/aboutus/Pages/QuickFactsaboutFLVS.aspx

Frankenberg, E., Siegel-Hawley, G., & Wang, J. (2010, January). *Choice without equity: Charter school segregation and the need for civil rights standards*. Los Angeles: The Civil Rights Project/Proyecto Derechos Civiles.

Friedman Foundation for Educational Choice. (2009). *The ABCs of school choice*. Indianapolis, IN: Author. Retrieved from http://www.edchoice.org/CMSModules/EdChoice/FileLibrary/394/ABCs_2008-9.pdf

Gardner, H. (1993). *The unschooled mind: How children think and how schools should teach*. New York: Basic Books.

Gewertz, C. (2009, November 20). Is house bill a preview of the "S" in ESEA? *Education Week*. Retrieved from http://blogs.edweek.org/edweek/high-school-connections/2009/11/graduation_promise_act.html

Gewertz, C. (2010, February 23). Experts lay out vision for future assessments: More-analytical tasks would replace factual recall of multiple-choice. *Education Week*, *29*(23), 8. Retrieved from http://www.edweek.org/ew/articles/2010/02/23/23assessment.h29.html

Goldstein, L. (2008, November). "Why are we learning this?": Experiential learning as a method of bolstering academic engagement and healthy identity development in middle school transition. Unpublished paper.

Goodlad, J. (2009, August 4). What are schools for? [blog post]. Forum for Education and Democracy. Retrieved from http://forumforeducation.org/node/487

G.O.P. platform on education and related issues. (1988, September 7). *Education Week*. Retrieved from http://www.edweek.org/ew/articles/1988/09/07/08370061.h08.html

Grabmeier, J. (2008, August 4). Ohio State study: Many "failing" schools aren't failing when measured on impact rather than achievement. Retrieved from http://www.osu.edu/news/newsitem2077

Hale, E. L., & Moorman, H. N. (2003). *Preparing school principals: A national perspective on policy and program innovations.* Washington, DC: Institute for Educational Leadership. Retrieved from http://www.iel.org/pubs/PreparingSchoolPrincipals.html

Harris Interactive. (2009). *The MetLife survey of the American teacher: Collaborating for student success.* Retrieved from http://www.metlife.com/about/corporate-profile/citizenship/metlife-foundation/metlife-survey-of-the-american-teacher.html

Hart, B., & Risley, T. (1995). *Meaningful differences in the everyday experience of young American children.* Baltimore: Paul H. Brookes.

Heckman, J. J. (2007, March 19). Beyond pre-K: Rethinking the conventional wisdom on educational intervention. *Education Week, 26*(28), 40. Retrieved from http://www.edweek.org/ew/articles/2007/03/19/28heckman.h26.html

Heckman, J. J., Moon, S. H., Pinto, R., Savelyev, P. A., & Yavitz, A. (2009, October). The rate of return to the High/Scope Perry Preschool Program. IZA Discussion Paper No. 4533. Bonn, Germany: The Institute for the Study of Labor (IZA).

Hodgkinson, H. L. (1999, June). All one system: A second look. In *Perspectives in public policy: Connecting higher education and the public schools* [Series]. The Institute for Educational Leadership and The National Center for Public Policy and Higher Education. Retrieved from http://208.112.118.116/images/All%20One%20System%20A%20Second%20Look%20pages%201-19.pdf

Hoff, D. J. (2008, December 19). School struggling to meet key goal on accountability. *Education Week, 8*(16), 1, 14–15. Retrieved from http://www.edweek.org/ew/articles/2008/12/18/16ayp.h28.html?tkn=WSUFINHdjng08OP46DYTNsqYVxzXPe6KEuX%2B&print=1

Holland, A. (Director), & Evans, S. (Producer). (2006). *A girl like me: The Gwen Araujo story* [Motion picture]. New York: A & E Television Networks (Lifetime Movie Network).

Horatio Alger Association of Distinguished Americans. (2005). *The state of our nation's youth.* Alexandria, VA: Author. Retrieved from http://www.horatioalger.com/pdfs/state05.pdf

Jordan, J. D. (2010, February 28). Teacher unions challenged in unprecedented face-off. *The Providence Journal.* Retrieved from http://www.projo.com/news/content/central_falls_turmoil_02-28-10_TQHGS9N_v292.38b0e26.html

Kolb, D. (1984). *Experiential learning: Experience as the source of learning and development.* Englewood Cliffs, NJ: Prentice-Hall.

Kolderie, T. (2005). *Ray Budde and the origins of the "charter concept"* [Paper]. St. Paul, MN: Education Evolving. Retrieved from http://www.educationevolving.org/pdf/Ray_Budde.pdf

Kolderie, T. (2010, April). *Innovation-based systemic reform: Getting beyond traditional school.* Education Evolving. Retrieved from http://www.educationevolving.org/pdf/Innovation-Based-Systemic-Reform.pdf

Krug, E. (1961, September). Charles W. Eliot and the secondary school. *History of Education Quarterly, 1*(3), 4–21.

Levin, J., Mulhern, J., & Schunck, J. (2005). *Unintended consequences: The case for reforming the staffing rules in urban teacher union contracts.* The New Teacher Project. Retrieved from http://www.tntp.org/files/UnintendedConsequences.pdf

Levin, J., & Quinn, M. (2003). *Missed opportunities: How we keep high-quality teachers out of urban classrooms.* The New Teacher Project. Retrieved from http://www.tntp.org/files/MissedOpportunities.pdf

Levine, A. (2006, September). *Educating school teachers.* The Education Schools Project. Retrieved from http://www.edschools.org/pdf/Educating_Teachers_Report.pdf

Littky, D., & Grabelle, S. (1994). *The big picture: Education is everyone's business.* Alexandria, VA: ASCD.

Lohr, S. (2009, August 19). Study finds that online education beats the classroom. *The New York Times.* Retrieved from http://bits.blogs.nytimes.com/2009/08/19/study-finds-that-online-education-beats-the-classroom/

LoMonaco, P. (2008, June 6). Tackling the dropout crisis comprehensively. *Education Week, 27*(41). Retrieved from http://www.edweek.org/ew/articles/2008/06/05/41lomonaco_web.h27.html

Long, A. (2004, April). Cyber schools. *ECS State Notes: Technology.* Denver, CO: Education Commission of the States.

Loveless, T. (2008, September). *The misplaced math student: Lost in eighth grade algebra.* Brown Center Report on American Education. Washington, DC: Brookings Institute.

Mackey, K. (2010, March). *Wichita Public Schools' learning centers: Creating a new educational model to serve dropouts and at-risk students.* Mountain View, CA: Innosight Institute. Retrieved from http://www.innosightinstitute.org/media-room/publications/education-publications/wichita-public-schools-learning-centers/

Macris, G. (2000, September 7). Gates grants praised. *Providence Journal-Bulletin.*

Manzo, K. K. (2006, May 22). Education schools inadequately prepare elementary teachers how to teach reading. *Education Week, 25.* Retrieved from http://www.edweek.org/ew/articles/2006/05/22/38read_web.h25.html

Manzo, K. K. (2009, March 24). Students see schools inhibiting their use of new technologies. *Education Week, 28*(27), 10. Retrieved from http://www.edweek.org/ew/articles/2009/03/24/27digital.h28.html

Marzano, R. J., & Kendall, J. S. (1998). *Awash in a sea of standards.* McRel. Retrieved from http://www.mcrel.org/PDF/Standards/5982IR_AwashInASea.pdf

Massachusetts 2020. (2010). *Expanded learning time initiative.* Retrieved from http://www.mass2020.org/node/10

Mathis, W. (2004, September). *What are we measuring: School quality or poverty?* National Education Association. Retrieved from http://www.nea.org/home/17622.htm

Matter of choice: The debate over schools and the marketplace. (1992, December 16). *Education Week.* Retrieved from http://www.edweek.org/ew/articles/1992/12/16/15choice.h12.html

McGrory, K. (2009, May 18). Costly plan failed to improve Miami schools. *Education Week, 28.* Retrieved from http://www.edweek.org/ew/articles/2009/05/18,/32mct_miami.html

McSpadden McNeil, L., Coppola, E., Radigan, J., & Vasquez Heilig, J. (2008). Avoidable losses: High-stakes accountability and the dropout crisis. *Education Policy Analysis Archives 2008.* Retrieved from http://epaa.asu.edu/ojs/article/view/28

McWalters, P. (2005, June). *The Rhode Island High School diploma system: All kids well-prepared for high performing, bright futures.* Brown University, The Education Alliance. Retrieved from http://www.ride.ri.gov/highschoolreform/docs/pdfs/high%20school%20reform/hsdiploma_v071405.pdf

Meloro, P. C. (2005). *Do high school advisory programs promote personalization? Correlates of school belonging.* ETD Collection for University of Rhode Island. Retrieved from http://digitalcommons.uri.edu/dissertations/AAI3188841

Meyer, J. P. (2008, December 21). Adams 50 skips grades, lets kids be pacesetters. *The Denver Post.* Retrieved from http://www.denverpost.com/news/ci_11280071

Miller, E., & Almon, J. (2009). *Crisis in the kindergarten: Why children need to play in school.* The Alliance for Childhood. Retrieved from http://drupal6.allianceforchildhood.org/sites/allianceforchildhood.org/files/file/kindergarten_report.pdf

Miller, L. S. (1995). *An American imperative: Accelerating minority educational advancement.* New Haven, CT: Yale University Press.

Moe, T., & Chubb, J. (2009). *Liberating learning: Technology, politics, and the future of American education.* San Francisco: Jossey-Bass.

National Association of Secondary School Principals. (1996). *Breaking ranks II and high school reform.* Brown University, The Education Alliance. Retrieved from http://www.principals.org/SchoolImprovement/BreakingRanksIIandHighSchoolReform.aspx

National Center for Education Statistics (NCES). (2009a). *Digest of education statistics: 2009.* Washington, DC: U.S. Department of Education. Retrieved from http://nces.ed.gov/pubsearch/pubsinfo.asp?pubid=2010013

National Center for Education Statistics (NCES). (2009b). *IPEDS graduation rate survey.* Washington, DC: U.S. Department of Education. Data retrieved from http://www.higheredinfo.org/dbrowser/index.php?submeasure=27&year=2008&level=nation&mode=graph&state=0

National Commission on Excellence in Education. (1983). *A nation at risk: The imperative for educational reform.* Washington, DC: U.S. Government Printing Office.

National Institute for Early Education Research (NIEER). (2007, November 8). *New report on preschool participation nationally highlights vast inequities.* Retrieved from http://nieer.org/mediacenter/index.php?PressID=78

National Mathematics Advisory Panel (NMAP). (2008). *Foundations for success: The final report of the National Mathematics Advisory Panel.* Washington, DC: U.S. Department of Education. Retrieved from http://www2.ed.gov/about/bdscomm/list/mathpanel/report/final-report.pdf

New Hampshire Department of Education. (2010). *Follow the child.* State of New Hampshire. Retrieved from http://www.education.nh.gov/innovations/follow_child/index.htm

New Jersey Department of Education. (2007, December). *A formula for success: All children, all communities.* Retrieved from http://www.state.nj.us/education/sff/reports/AllChildrenAllCommunities.pdf

Newell, R. J. (2003). *Passion for learning: How project-based learning meets the needs of the 21st century students.* Lanham, MD: Rowman and Littlefield Education.

Oakes, J., & Saunders, M. (2009, July 20). Multiple pathways: Bringing school to life. *Education Week, 28*(37). Retrieved from http://www.edweek.org/ew/articles/2009/07/20/37oakes.h28.html

Office of Educational Technology, U.S. Department of Education. (2010, March 5). *Transforming American education: Learning powered by technology. Draft: National Educational Technology Plan 2010.* Retrieved from http://www2.ed.gov/about/offices/list/os/technology/netp.pdf

Olson, L. (2005). Financial evolution. *Education Week, 24*(17), 8–12, 14. Retrieved from http://www.edweek.org/ew/articles/2005/01/06/17overview.h24.html?qs=jacob+adams+Public_school_finance_systems

Organization for Economic Cooperation and Development. (2008). *Measuring improvements in learning outcomes: Best practices to assess the value-added of schools.*

Parsad, B., & Lewis, L. (2003). *Remedial education at degree-granting postsecondary institutions in fall 2000.* NCES 2004-010. Washington, DC: U.S. Department of Education, National Center for Education Statistics.

Patrick, S. (2010). National online and blended learning landscape. [PowerPoint presentation]. International Association for K-12 Online Learning. Retrieved from http://www.k12blueprint.com/k12/blueprint/cd/visionary2010_susan_patrick.pdf

Phelps, R. (Ed.). (2005). *Defending standardized testing.* Mahwah, NJ: Lawrence Erlbaum Associates.

Phelps, R. (2006). *Estimating the costs and benefits of educational testing programs.* Education Consumers Clearinghouse. Retrieved from http://www.education-consumers.com/briefs/phelps2.shtm

Pre-K Now. (n.d.). The benefits of high-quality pre-K. [Fact sheet]. Retrieved from http://www.preknow.org/advocate/factsheets/benefits.cfm

Prensky, M. (2001, October). Digital natives, digital immigrants: A new way to look at ourselves and our kids. *On the Horizon, 9*(5). MCB University Press. Retrieved from http://www.marcprensky.com/writing/Prensky%20-%20Digital%20Natives,%20Digital%20Immigrants%20-%20Part1.pdf

Quint, J. C., Smith, J. K., Unterman, R., & Moedano, A. E. (2010, February). *New York City's changing high school landscape: High schools and their*

characteristics, 2002–2008. New York: MDRC. Retrieved from http://www
.mdrc.org/publications/543/full.pdf

Raudenbush, S. W. (2004, April 1). *Schooling, statistics, and poverty: Can we
measure school improvement?* Educational Testing Service. Retrieved from
http://www.ets.org/Media/Education_Topics/pdf/angoff9.pdf

Ravitch, D. (2010). *The death and life of the great American school system: How
testing and choice are undermining education.* New York: Basic Books.

Ravitch, D. (2010, March 9). Why I changed my mind about school reform: Federal testing has narrowed education and charter schools have failed to live
up to their promise. *The Wall Street Journal.* Retrieved from http://online
.wsj.com/article/SB10001424052748704869304575109443305343962.html

Rebell, M. A., & Baker, B. D. (2009, July 8). Assessing "success" in school finance
litigations. *Education Week, 28*(36). Retrieved from http://www.edweek.org/
ew/articles/2009/07/08/36rebell.h28.html

Roach, R. (2010, January 27). Minority male plight demands broad U.S.
action, College Board says. EducationNews.org. Retrieved from http://www
.educationnews.org/educationnewstoday/36329.html

Robinson, K. (2005, July 14). Presentation by Sir Ken Robinson. *The Education
Commission of the States 2005 National Forum of Education Policy Chair-
man's Breakfast.* Retrieved from http://www.ecs.org/html/projectsPartners/
Chair2005/docs/Sir_Ken_Robinson_Speech.pdf

Schmoker, M. (2008, December/2009, January). Measuring what matters. *Educational Leadership, 66*(4), 70–74. Retrieved from http://
performanceassessment.org/articles/measuringwhatmatters.pdf

Schools Matter. (2006, November 16). Sandy Kress at the feeding trough redux.
Retrieved from http://www.schoolsmatter.info/2006/11/sandy-kress-at-
feeding-trough-redux.html

Schroeder, J. (2004). *Ripples of innovation.* Washington, DC: Progressive
Policy Institute. Retrieved from http://www.ppionline.org/documents/
MN_Charters_0504.pdf

Schweinhart, L. J., Montie, J., Xiang, Z., Barnett, W. S., Belfield, C. R., & Nores, M.
(2005). *Lifetime effects: The HighScope Perry Preschool study through age 40.*
Ypsilanti, MI: HighScope Press. Retrieved from http://www.highscope.org/
content.asp?contentid=219

Science Daily. (2009, February 1). College freshmen in US and China: Chinese
students know more science facts but neither group especially skilled in
reasoning. *Science Daily.* Retrieved from http://www.sciencedaily.com/
releases/2009/01/090129140840.htm

Steenhuysen, J. (2010, February 16). Many U.S. kids have chronic health
problem: Study. Reuters. Retrieved from http://www.reuters.com/
article/idUSTRE61F58520100216

Stillwell, R. (2010). *Public school graduates and dropouts from the common core of
data: School year 2007–08* (NCES 2010-341). Washington, DC: U.S. Department
of Education, National Center for Education Statistics. Retrieved September
14, 2010, from http://nces.ed.gov/pubsearch/pubsinfo.asp?pubid=2010341

Tanner, D., & Tanner, L. (1995). *Curriculum development: Theory into practice.* Englewood Cliffs, NJ: Prentice-Hall.

Thomas, D. (2007, August). *Co-op history.* EdVisions Cooperative. Retrieved from http://edvisionscooperative.org/about/history

Thomas, D. (n.d.). *History of MNCS: Little did we know: Ten years in the making of the Minnesota New Country School.* Retrieved from http://newcountryschool.com/default.asp

Time, Learning, and Afterschool Task Force. (2007). *A new day for learning.* Flint, MI: C. S. Mott Foundation. Retrieved from http://www.newdayforlearning.org/docs/NDL_Jan07.pdf

USCharterSchools.org. (n.d.). State information. Retrieved from www.uscharterschools.org/pub/uscs_docs/sp/index.htm

U.S. Department of Education. (n.d.). 10 facts about K–12 education funding. Retrieved from http://www2.ed.gov/about/overview/fed/10facts/index.html

U.S. Department of Labor. (2009, December 17). *Occupational Outlook Handbook, 2010–11 Edition.* Retrieved from http://www.bls.gov/oco/oco2003.htm#education

Viadero, D. (2009, March 6). Algebra-for-all policy found to raise rates of failure in Chicago. *Education Week, 28*(24), 11. Retrieved from http://www.edweek.org/ew/articles/2009/03/11/24algebra.h28.html

Viadero, D. (2010, February 9). "Algebra-for-all" push found to yield poor results. *Education Week, 29*(21), 1, 14. Retrieved from http://www.edweek.org/ew/articles/2010/02/10/21algebra_ep.h29.html

Wall Street Journal. (2006, September 22). No teacher left behind. Retrieved from http://www.edschools.org/news/Wall_Street_Journal_092206.htm

Walsh, M. (2002, June 27). Supreme Court upholds Cleveland voucher program. *Education Week.* Retrieved from http://www.edweek.org/ew/articles/2002/06/27/42voucher_web.h21.html

Washor, E., Mojkowski, C., & Foster, D. (2009, March). Living literacy: A cycle of life to text and text to life. *Phi Delta Kappan, 90*(7), 521–523. Retrieved from http://www.bigpicture.org/wpcontent/uploads/2009/03/livingliteracy_kappan.pdf

Wilensky, R. (2007, December). High schools have got it bad for higher ed—And that ain't good. *Phi Delta Kappan, 89*(4), 248–256, 258–259. Retrieved from http://www.pdkintl.org/kappan/k_v89/k0712toc.htm

Williams, B., & Menounos, M. (Creators). (2009, November 27). *Connecticut teens to the rescue: NBC nightly news* [Television broadcast]. NBC Universal Inc. Retrieved from http://icue.nbcunifiles.com/icue/files/nbcarchives/site/pdf/48674.pdf

Wolk, R. (2001, August 17). Exam anxiety. *Teacher Magazine, 13*(1), 4. Retrieved from http://www.edweek.org/tm/articles/2001/08/17/01persp.h13.html?qs=ronald+wolk+and+rigorous

Wraga, W. (2009). Toward a connected core curriculum. *Educational Horizons, Pi Lambda Theta, 87*(2), 88–96. Retrieved from http://www.pilambda.org/horizons/v87-2/wraga.pdf

| INDEX |

| ABOUT THE AUTHOR |

 During his career, Ron Wolk has kept one foot in journalism and the other in education. He spent 10 years as assistant to President Milton S. Eisenhower at Johns Hopkins University and 10 years at Brown University as vice president of external affairs. He was a staff member on the Carnegie Commission on the Future of Higher Education and later on the National Commission on the Causes and Prevention of Violence.

As president of Editorial Projects in Education, Wolk is the founder and former editor of *Education Week, Teacher Magazine,* and *Quality Counts.*

After more than two decades of work in the school reform trenches, Ron retired in 1997 and moved to Rhode Island, where he has remained active in trying to improve public education. He is chairman of Big Picture Learning, an organization devoted to creating small, innovative schools.

In 2008, the Education Commission of the States awarded Wolk the James Bryant Conant Award for his notable contributions to education.

Related ASCD Resources: School Reform

At the time of publication, the following ASCD resources were available (ASCD stock numbers appear in parentheses). For up-to-date information about ASCD resources, go to www.ascd.org.

ASCD Professional Interest Communities

Exchange ideas and connect with other educators interested in restructuring schools on the social networking site ASCD EDge™ at http://ascdedge .ascd.org.

Print Products

Align the Design: A Blueprint for School Improvement by Nancy J. Mooney and Ann T. Mausbach (#108005)

The Big Picture: Education Is Everyone's Business by Dennis Littky and Samantha Grabelle (#104438)

Breaking Free from Myths About Teaching and Learning: Innovation as an Engine for Student Success by Allison Zmuda (#109041)

Education Unbound: The Promise and Practice of Greenfield Schooling by Frederick M. Hess (#109040)

Leading Change in Your School: How to Conquer Myths, Build Commitment, and Get Results by Douglas B. Reeves (#109019)

Results Now: How We Can Achieve Unprecedented Improvements in Teaching and Learning by Mike Schmoker (#106045)

For more information: send e-mail to member@ascd.org; call 1-800-933-2723 or 703-578-9600, press 2; send a fax to 703-575-5400; or write to Information Services, ASCD, 1703 N. Beauregard St., Alexandria, VA 22311-1714 USA.